Contents

Introduction

BY HENRI LOYRETTE

PRESIDENT AND DIRECTOR OF THE LOUVRE MUSEUM

Visiting or revisiting the Louvre is always an ambitious undertaking—you couldn't discover all the masterpieces in the world's largest and best-known museum even if you had three full days. So what is the best way to approach this labyrinthine palace, this encyclopedia of universal art, whose collections—which span a timeframe from 8000 BC to 1848—hold so much in store?

This illustrated issue, published by the Louvre Museum in conjunction with *Beaux Arts magazine*, offers a diverse and attractive approach to the collection for visitors who don't want to miss any of the masterpieces. It aims to allay the legitimate concerns of those who find the breadth and range of this prestigious collection of art somewhat challenging.

Through a selection of major works, with texts by the museum curators, readers can discover or rediscover the known and lesser-known masterpieces in the Louvre's departments: treasures from Antiquity, drawings, paintings, the decorative arts, sculptures and more.

This publication is also an opportunity to present new developments within these departments. The collection is constantly growing as a result of ongoing efforts to acquire new works of art. We are maintaining and pursuing this long-standing acquisitions policy, which has created the museum's diversity that began with the royal collections of the Renaissance and continues to this day. The expansion of the museum's collection is also the result of new policy decisions and recent initiatives, such as the exhibition of art from Africa, Asia, Oceania and the Americas in 2000, and the inauguration of the Department of Islamic Art in 2003—both of which represent a turning point in terms of other arts and traditions. In 2005, the historic Tuileries gardens became part of the Louvre, extending the museum to the Place de la Concorde. The result of a long secular history, the Louvre is above all a museum that looks to the future.

The introduction of contemporary art within its walls reflects this new dialogue between artists, the artwork and the public—a confirmation that the Louvre remains a source of inspiration for us all.

HISTORY OF THE LOUVRE

BY Geneviève Bresc-Bautier

Head curator, in charge of the Department of Sculpture

∧ 1. CHARLES MEYNIER
(1768-1832)

THE TRIUMPH OF FRENCH PAINTING: THE APOTHEOSIS OF POUSSIN, LE SUEUR AND LE BRUN

Oil on canvas, 81 x 36 cm, commissioned in 1820.

The historical rooms in the Louvre exhibit a major series of sketches painted for the Louvre ceilings or sculpted for the exterior décor. Here, the project for the Duchâtel Room, decorated in 1820; it was an extension to the staircase constructed by Percier and Fontaine and served as the vestibule for the Salon Carré.

facing page

< 2. HUBERT ROBERT
(1733-1808)

THE GRANDE GALERIE OF THE LOUVRE IN 1794-1796

Circa 1801–1805, oil on canvas, 37 x 46 cm.

The Comte d'Angiviller wanted to open a museum in the Grande Galerie to exhibit the royal painting collection. Hubert Robert, an artist and Keeper of the King's Paintings from 1784 to 1792 who lived in the Louvre, painted proposals for the museum layout, with both realistic and imaginary views of the various rooms.

Eight centuries separate Philippe Auguste's late twelfth-century fortress from Ieoh Ming Pei's pyramid, built in 1989. The Louvre's medieval château, remnants of which are still visible, was transformed into a lavish Renaissance residence; the Salle des Cariatides and the façade of the Cour Carré are testimonies to its inventive design. Henri IV imagined a "Grand Dessein" for the palace, a royal city, and erected the Grande Galerie along the banks of the Seine. It linked the Louvre to the Palais des Tuileries, which Catherine de Médicis had constructed just outside the city walls. Louis XIII then commissioned Poussin to decorate the Grande Galerie and undertook a project to quadruple the size of the Cour Carrée. And before Louis XIV moved the royal court to Versailles, he had transformed the Louvre into the first laboratory of classical art, where Bernini's projects were absorbed into the classic monumentality of Claude Perrault's imposing colonnade. The major participants in Louis XIV's project all left their mark: the buildings by architect Le Vau; the Apollo Gallery project (now reopened to its original splendor after a major renovation) by the painter Le Brun; and the re-landscaping of the Tuileries gardens by Le Nôtre, who created a magnificent illusionist perspective.

The Louvre had also become a palace of the arts. Henri IV housed his artists on the premises and displayed his collection of antiques here, while Louis XIV adapted the building for his academies, as well as the Cabinet des Tableaux and Salle des Antiques. Under the impetus of Enlightenment philosophers, Louis XVI planned to create a "Muséum," which was inaugurated during the Revolution on August 10, 1793. The collection grew with works from the royal collections and from artwork confiscated from churches and emigrants. It then expanded considerably with the European conquests of the Directory, followed by those of

the Empire. With the "Musée Napoléon," the Louvre's Grand Dessein was revived, as evidenced by the Arc de Triomphe du Carrousel, the north wing and the staircases. But the plundered works were returned after the fall of the Empire.

During the Restoration, the museum compensated for gaps in the collection by actively pursuing acquisitions, decorating rooms and opening new sections. These included a sculpture gallery, the Musée Charles X, devoted to Egyptian art (through Champollion's efforts), Greek vases and the Musée de la Marine featuring a wealth of objects from Oceania and the Americas. Assyrian art entered the Louvre with the arrival of the *Winged Assyrian Bulls of Khorsabad*. The Grand Dessein was resuscitated once again during the Second Republic, under Napoleon III. In 1857, the architects Visconti and Lefuel linked the Louvre to the Palais des Tuileries. New buildings around the Cour Napoleon and lavishly decorated spaces (the Salle du Manège, the Napoleon III apartments, staircases) were created to meet the needs of a site that served as both a museum and royal residence (the Palais des Tuileries since 1789). In 1871, the Palais des Tuileries was burned to the ground by the Commune, opening up the view to the western areas of Paris. The collection continued to grow throughout the Third Republic, as the museum gradually occupied more and more of the buildings. Despite an ambitious plan in the 1930s, which continued through the 1970s thanks to André Malraux, the works remained in cramped quarters. The "Grand Louvre" program, launched in 1981, completely restructured the museum: the pyramid and underground entrance were constructed, and once the Richelieu Wing became part of the museum, the collection was entirely rearranged. Year after year, new rooms and new wings, designed according to an ambitious and effective museum program, are opening to the public.

3. JOSEPH AUGUSTE
**THE JEWEL ROOM AND
THE MUSÉE CHARLES X ROOMS**

Circa 1835, oil on canvas, 100 x 81 cm.

The collection of Decorative Arts from the Middle Ages and the Renaissance, exhibited in the former Grand Cabinet du Roi in large display cases designed by the architect Fontaine. To the right: The Virgin by Jeanne d'Évreux, Charles X's Shield; to the left, a silver statue of Henri IV by Bosio.

4. ANGE TISSIER
(1814-1876)
**THE ARCHITECT VISCONTI PRESENTING
THE PLANS FOR THE NEW LOUVRE
TO THE SOVEREIGNS**

1865, oil on canvas, 178 x 231 cm. Acquired in 1866.

This painting depicts the architect Louis Visconti, who died in December of 1853, presenting a gigantic plan of the New Louvre to the imperial couple, in a room of the Palais des Tuileries. This official version, presented to the Salon of 1866, is historically incorrect, because Eugénie had not yet married Napoleon when the project was proposed.

5. GIUSEPPE DE NITTIS
(1846-1884)
**THE PLACE DU CARROUSEL,
THE RUINS OF THE PALAIS DES TUILERIES**

1882, oil on wood, 45 x 60 cm.
Acquired in 1883.

Italian painter De Nittis created a poetic image of the burnt hulk of the Palais des Tuileries just before it was torn down. Shacks were built around the Place du Carrousel. The Pavillon de Marsan to the right had already been reconstructed by Hector-Martin Lefuel to house the Cour des Comptes.

6. FRANÇOIS BIARD
(1798-1882)
FOUR O-CLOCK IN THE SALON [DETAIL]
1847, oil on canvas, 57 x 67 cm.
Gift from Mortimer Schiff, 1921.

Biard created a lighthearted painting of the 1845 Salon, as the painting was exhibited at the last Salon held in the Louvre, in 1847. A socially diverse Parisian public flocked to the Grande Galerie, where the works were hung frame to frame on the walls. The guards, wearing royal livery, announce the closing of the gallery.

Department of

NEAR EASTERN ANTIQUITIES

BY ANNIE CAUBET
HONORARY CHIEF CURATOR

The Department of Near Eastern Antiquities is devoted to the early civilizations of the Near and Middle East, beginning with the first settlements that appeared about 10,000 years ago. The pieces are exhibited according to their geographic origins: Mesopotamia, Iran, the Levant and the "Arabia Felix" (modern-day Yemen). Despite the immense area and diverse civilizations that flourished throughout this long period, they shared a number of common traits. The first is the existence of a family of languages, some dating from 5,000 years ago: Akkadian, Babylonian, Phoenician, Aramaic, Hebrew and Arabic. The second concerns the environment and the necessity of adapting to it. The oldest cities developed in the valleys of the Nile, in Egypt; in the Ganges and the Indus in India; and in the double valley of the Tigris and the Euphrates, or Mesopotamia, in the Near East. The latter two rivers formed the "fertile crescent," an immense bow that linked the banks of the Mediterranean Sea to the Persian Gulf. This is where mankind first domesticated plants and animals during the Neolithic period, in the eighth millennium BC. Nomadic hunters became sedentary and settled into villages. With the development of city-states, the increasingly complex economies required a method for keeping accounts.

Hence writing was born, around 3300 BC, in the land of Sumer, in the southern areas of the Tigris and Euphrates valley (modern-day Iraq). Several empires developed during the third, second and first millennia BC: the Empires of Ur, Akkadian, Babylonian, Hittite, Assyrian and Elamist in southwest Iran; and the merchant kingdoms of the Levant, including Mari in the Middle Euphrates and Ugarit on the Syrian coast. In the wake of Alexander's conquest, the Near East came under Greek, then Roman rule, and many people converted to Christianity, although this religion's

rapid expansion did not hinder the growth of Judaism in Palestine and Syria. After the crisis of the Byzantine Empire came the Arab conquest and the Islamization of the Mediterranean area. This religion tolerated large and prosperous Jewish and Christian communities in their midst, many of which are still thriving to this day. The modern Western world inherited a dual culture through the written sources that sprung in the Near East: the biblical tradition on the one hand, and the Greco-Roman traditions on the other. The Jews were exiled from their lands in the Near East to Babylon during the sixth century BC; they then assimilated the Mesopotamian intellectual milieu dating from the third millennium BC. After Alexander the Great's conquest, by the late fourth century BC the entire Near East was speaking Greek, while retaining the heritage of its ancient philosophies. This was bequeathed to intellectuals of mixed culture, such as Flavius Josephus, a Greek-speaking Jewish historian, and Lucian of Samosata, who wrote *Dialogue of the Gods* in Greek. Hellenized oriental writers, theologians, philosophers and mathematicians therefore helped to keep millennia-old traditions alive to this day, despite the fact that the civilizations that created them have completely disappeared. The Department of Near Eastern Antiquities was created in 1881. The archeological collection was formed primarily from the nineteenth century through the Second World War. It presents a complete overview of these different civilizations, thanks to excavations undertaken on numerous archeological sites. The first of these, at Khorsabad, dates to 1843–1854, and brought to light the Assyrian culture and the forgotten civilizations of the Near East. The goal of the Louvre, which played a key role in this rediscovery of Near Eastern history, is to show the depth of its cultural roots and the enduring values of the Near East to the public of today.

facing page

1. WINGED ASSYRIAN BULLS

Assyrian Empire, reign of Sargon II (721–705 BC), Khorsabad, ancient Dur-Sharrukin, Assyria, Iraq, gypseous alabaster, 420 x 436 cm.

These monumental sculptures are protective spirits that guarded the gates of the capital and the palace, constructed for the glory of the Assyrian king Sargon ii. The human-headed winged bull was a benevolent spirit that was part of Mesopotamia mythology from the third millennium BC on.

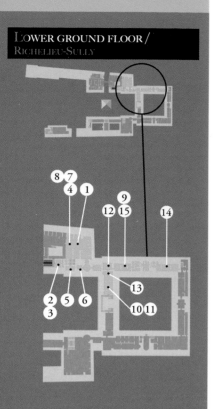

LOWER GROUND FLOOR /
RICHELIEU-SULLY

< 2. TABLET OF PRE-CUNEIFORM
SCRIPT

Uruk III (3100-2900 BC), Mésopotamie, Iraq, clay,
4.5 x 4.3 x 2.4 cm.

This tablet, one of the oldest in existence, is covered with pictographs, which represented the earliest form of writing. The invention of writing around 3300 BC coincided with the development of more complex societies that required systems for recording and transmitting information.

3. STELE OF THE VULTURES >

Protodynastic III (2600–2330), Tello, ancient
Girsu, Sumer, Iraq, limestone, 180 x 130 x 11 cm.

The "Stele of the Vultures," the first historical monument recording a victory, shows Enna-tum, the Sumerian prince of Lagash around 2450 BC, triumph over his adversaries while the vultures pick at the corpses of the dead soldiers.

< 4. VICTORY STELE
OF NARAM-SIN

Akkad Dynasty, reign of Naram-Sin (2254–
2218 BC), discovered at Susa, Iran; originally from
Mesopotamia, Iraq, pink sandstone, 200 x 105 cm.

The stele commemorates the victory of the Akkadian king Naram-Sin over the Lullubi, a mountain people from the region of central Zagros. The battle takes place in a mountainous landscape depicting the Akkadian army following their sovereign up a hill. The defeated soldiers are hiding behind trees clinging to the hillside.

facing page

5. EBIH-IL, THE SUPERINTENDENT
OF MARI >

Protodynastic III (2600–2330 BC), Mari, Northern
Mesopotamia, Syria, alabaster, shell, lapis lazuli,
bitumen, 52.5 x 20.6 x 30 cm.

The exceptionally beautiful statue depicts a leading figure from the kingdom of Mari. An inscription engraved on his shoulder gives his name, Ebih-il, and his rank of superintendent. The eyes are made of lapis lazuli, a stone imported from Afghanistan; they are outlined in bitumen and set in a shell.

< 6. BEAKER DECORATED WITH WADING BIRDS, DOGS AND IBEX

Susa I, c. 4200–3500 BC, Susa, Iran, painted terracotta, 28.9 x 16.4 cm.

This tall vase belonged to the funerary offerings placed in the Susa necropolis during the first period of the city. It was used to hold the bones of the deceased. The extremely elaborate and organized compositions and boldly stylized design are characteristic of ceramics produced during this period. Desert dogs and wading birds decorate the sides.

< 7. GUDEA, PRINCE OF LAGASH

Circa 2120 BC, Tello, ancient Girsu, diorite, 70 x 22.4 cm.

This statue is one of the many effigies of Gudea, Sumerian prince of the state of Lagash in the late 22nd century BC. Gudea was an extremely pious prince whose primary concern was the construction and restoration of his state's major sanctuaries in the Sumerian tradition, after the fall of the Akkadian Empire.

< 8. CODE OF HAMMURABI [DETAIL]

First Babylonian Dynasty, reign of Hammurabi (1792–1750 BC), discovered at Susa, Iran, origin: Mesopotamia, Iraq, basalt, 225 x 190 cm.

This basalt stele is inscribed with the first known list of laws. It includes a prologue and sentences divided into 282 articles governing the primary aspects of society. The scene at the top depicts a meeting between the sovereign of Babylon—the defender of the weak against the strong, of orphans and widows—and the sun god Shamash, who is handing the emblems of universal power to the king.

facing page

9. THE GARDS OF DARIUS >

Achemenide-Persian dynasty, 522–486 BC, Susa, Iran, glazed bricks, 475 x 375 cm (each brick: 8.5 x 33 x 17 cm).

Each of these soldiers carries a bow, a quiver and a spear. Clad in long robes and adorned with jewelry, they once decorated the walls of Darius I's palace in Susa. They illustrate the grandeur and power of the Achemenide Persian Empire, which renewed the architectural inventions of Babylon, as, for example, the Ishtar Gate.

< 10. GOLD PLATE
WITH HUNTING SCENE

14th–13th century BC, Ras Shamra, ancient Ugarit,
near the Temple of Baal, Mediterranean coast, Syria,
gold, diam.: 18.8 cm, height: 3 cm.

*This gold plate comes from the acropolis of Ugarit.
The design shows a chariot driven by the king, who
is armed with a bow accompanied by his dogs in his
pursuit of wild bulls and goats. The genre of hunting
scenes symbolizes the struggle against the forces
of evil, and represents the king as the upholder of
the established order.*

11. STATUE OF QUEEN NAPIR-ASU,
WIFE OF UNTASH-NAPIRISHA >

Higihalkide Dynasty, reign of Untash-Napirisha,
14th century BC, Susa, Iran, bronze, copper,
129 x 73 cm.

*The statue of Queen Napir-Asu, one of the largest
bronze sculptures from the ancient Near East, is a
monumental and imposing piece of work. She was
the wife of Untash-Napirisha, a king from the
Middle Elamite period. It is one of the very few
portrayals of female royalty from the 2nd
millennium.*

< 12. STELE OF
THE WEATHER-GOD BAAL

13th century BC, Ras Shamra, ancient Ugarit,
near the Temple of Baal, Mediterranean coast,
Syria, sandstone, 142 x 50 x 28 cm.

*Baal appears here in the pose of a fighting god,
armed with a sword and brandishing his mace,
a symbol of thunder. Vegetation, a result of the
beneficial effects of rain, grows from the tip of his
spear. He ruled over the earth's fertility and
protected the king, places under his arm.*

∧ 13. STATUE FROM AIN GHAZAL

8th millennium, PPNB period, Ain Ghazal,
Jordan, gypsum plaster, 105 cm. On loan from the
Jordan Department of Antiquities.

*This statue was modeled from gypsum plaster
over an skeleton of reeds and braided twine. It
was discovered on the site of Ain Ghazal, a large
village from the PPNB era (Pre Pottery Neolithic
B, according to terminology established on the
nearby site of Jericho), when agricultural communities developed rapidly in the Near East.*

∧ 14. TRIAD OF PALMYRENAN GODS

First half of the 1st century AD, near Bir Wereb,
Palmyra, Syria, limestone, 69 x 56 cm.

*This work represents the supreme god Baalshamin
(he who brings rain), between the moon god
Aglibol to his right and the sun god Malakbel
(Yarhibol) to his left. These were the most important gods in the rich trading city of Palmyra. They
are all wearing Roman-style armor over Persian-
style trousers and tunics.*

∧ 15. LEAPING WINGED IBEX

Vase handle, Achemenides-Persian dynasty,
539–333 BC, Iran, silver, gold, height: 26.5 cm.

*The rear legs of this animal, which itself forms the
handle of a vase, rise from a mask of Silenus. It
illustrates the high degree of craftsmanship achieved
by goldsmiths during the Persian era. They combined
the traditions of Near Eastern animal art with
motifs inspired from Greek and Egyptian art.*

Department of
ISLAMIC ART

BY FRANCIS RICHARD

HEAD CURATOR

∧ 1. BOWL WITH STANDARD BEARER

Iraq, 10th century, earthenware, metallic luster glaze, diam.: 31.8 cm. Former Alphonse Kann Collection, Gift from Michel Maurice-Bokanowski, 1949.

This bowl illustrates the power and wealth of the Abbasid Empire as well as the expertise of its potters. The words "al-mulk" (sovereignty) are written on the standard. The gilded tones of the glaze, created with silver and copper oxides among other materials, make this an object of luxury.

facing page

< 2. PYXIS OF AL-MUGHIRA

Spain, Madinat al-Zahra, 968, ivory, carved and engraved décor, height: 15 cm, diam.: 8 cm. Former Riano Collection. Acquired in 1898.

This object, a masterpiece in ivory art from the caliphate of Cordoba, may have been designed to hold perfumes or jewels. It was a gift to al-Mughira, the son of Caliph Abd al-Rahman III. The decoration illustrates scenes from the court: figures seated on thrones, hunting and music.

Although the Louvre's Department of Islamic Art was formed recently (in 2003), its origins are much older, and some of the objects were even part of the royal collection. Early on, in 1890, the Louvre created a section devoted to Islamic art, which was included in the Department of Decorative Arts; it consisted of a number of works collected by Émile Molinier and Gaston Migeon. Specific rooms opened in 1905 and again in 1922, providing the public with the opportunity to discover these works. The Islamic section, which became part of the Department of Oriental Antiquities in 1945, was rearranged with the Grand Louvre project in 1993. The works are exhibited in a more satisfactory way, and visitors can discover a selection of works in thirteen rooms of the Richelieu Wing that reflect the artistic production of most of the dynasties that predominated in the Muslim world, from the origins of Islam to the early twentieth century. By 2008, the department will have more rooms. In addition to the pieces now in the Louvre, a large number of works will be loaned by the Musée des Arts Décoratifs, whose collection—including exceptional carpets and ceramics—perfectly complement that of the Louvre.

The current itinerary is essentially chronological. The visit begins with a presentation of objects from Susa (Iran), illustrating the various activities of a city at the beginning of the Muslim expansion. Faience and ceramics with metallic luster glazes (*Bowl with Standard Bearer*) present the diversity of the Abbasid civilization. Delicate ivory and wooden objects from Egypt evoking the second caliphate and works dating from the early centuries of Islam in Syria illustrate the refinement of the diverse Abbasid culture. A few works present the Spanish art of the caliphs, notably the famous ivory *Pyxis of al-Mughira*. Central Asia during the tenth and eleventh centuries is represented by objects such as the *Shroud of Saint Josse*. Ceramics and metals from medieval Iranian provinces featuring various shapes and with highly diverse decorative motifs follow. Room VI is devoted to Iran under the Seljuk rulers (eleventh–thirteenth centuries) and to masterful works such as the *Falconer Bowl*, the *Cock's-Head Ewer* and the *Lion Perfume-Burner*, alongside extremely beautiful ceramics featuring calligraphy and magnificent décors, similar to the metalwork from this period. Also noteworthy is the beautiful *Royal Head*, which probably comes from Rayy. Next is a selection of objects linked to the sciences and to writing, with various instruments, including the famous *Celestial Sphere* from 1145. After a display devoted to an Egyptian cemetery, complete with steles, visitors discover works from Asia Minor, Syria and Egypt in Room VIII, with the famous *Barberini Vase* and the *Bowl with the Arms of Baybar*. After viewing the *Baptistery of Saint Louis*, visitors enter the Mameluke room containing a collection of lamps, large metal pieces and a key from the Kaaba with gold and silver inlays. Next is the section devoted to Mongolian Iran, with a display of extraordinary tiles, metal objects and ceramics. Room XI contains masterpieces of Timurid, Safavid and Qajar art; and a selection of weapons and works from Mughal India, including superb jades, a few fabrics and several carpets. Room XII is devoted to Ottoman art: alongside magnificent Iznik ceramics, such as the *Peacock Plate*, panels from the mausoleum of Selim II (1577) and the Rusem Pasha mosque, visitors can admire a carpet with medallions from Ushak and a jade bowl inlaid with gold and rubies that belonged to Louis XIV. Finally, a few pages of manuscripts and notebooks, exhibited on a rotating basis, remind visitors that the Louvre has a world-renowned collection of these objects.

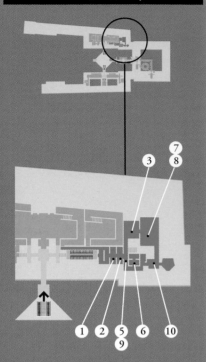

< 3. PEACOCK PLATE

Turkey, Iznik, 1540–1555, ceramic, underglaze painted decoration, diam.: 37.5 cm.
Raymond Koechlin bequest, 1932.

The whimsical and realistic, but poetic Saz-style foliage came from Central Asia and Iran and was reworked by miniaturists in the imperial Ottoman painting studios. This décor fills the space, while the alternating light and dark tones create a background that sets off the peacock.

4. AKBAR AND JAHANGIR WITH SUFIS AND YOGIS >

Page of a notebook signed by Payag, India, c. 1650–1660, gouache and gold on paper, 55.6 x 35 cm. Acquired in 2004.

Payag, a painter in the imperial Mughal work-shops, excelled at nocturnal scenes. Jahangir, seated behind his father Akbar, is participating in a discussion with Muslim and Hindu mystics. Emperor Akbar was interested in all religions and met often with Christian missionaries.

< 5. SHROUD OF SAINT JOSSE

Iran, Khurasan, before 961, silk, main piece: 94 x 52 cm, from a reliquary from the former Saint Josse Abbey (Pas-de-Calais). Acquired in 1922.

This fabric belonged to a Turkish emir from eastern Iran prior to 961 and may have tran-sited via Byzantium. In the early 12th century, it protected the relics of Saint Josse, thanks to a gift from Étienne de Blois, king of England, who was allied to Godefroy de Bouillon and Baudouin de Jérusalem, leading figures of the first crusade.

6. ROYAL HEAD >

Iran, Rayy?, early 13th century, stucco, traces of paint,
25 x 16 cm. Former Jean Soustiel Collection.
Acquired in 1999.

This head of a young prince was discovered in the ruins
of a palace that was probably destroyed by the Mongols
sometime around 1256. The full, serene face; the small,
slightly smiling mouth; and traces of the pink complex-
ion are all in keeping with the poetic canons of Iranian
art.

7. MANTES CARPET

Northwest Iran, late 16th century, wool, asymmetric
knots, 783 x 379 cm, from the Notre-Dame de Mantes-la-
Jolie collegiate church (Yvelines). Acquired in 1912.

The carpet includes a millennium-old theme of the
primordial pond; a poetic touch with a flowering shrub
entwined around a cypress, a symbol of lovers; and an
unexpected intrusion of modernity, a hunter with a
musket. Dragons and a phoenix, motifs that had been
adopted by Iranian artists centuries earlier, add a
Chinese note.

facing page

8. "FOUR-MIRROR" ARMOR >

India or Iran, 17th–18th century, steel, engraved and gilded décor, height: 86 cm. Baroness Salomon de Rothschild bequest, 1922.

The brilliant four plates protecting the torso, highlighted by the gilded décor, explain the name of this type of armor, which was used in the Safavid Empire in Iran, the Mughal Empire in India and the Ottoman Empire. The overall suit, including helmet, coat of mail and armbands, was relatively lightweight.

< 9. CELESTIAL SPHERE

Iran, Isfahan, 1145, brass, engraved with silver inlays, diam.: 16.5 cm. Acquired in 1985.

All the constellations described by the Greek scholar Ptolemy in the 2nd century appear on the globe, but the positions were recalculated and correspond to the locations in the sky ten centuries later. This is the oldest known celestial sphere from the eastern regions of the Muslim world.

< 10. BASIN KNOWN AS THE BAPTISTERY OF SAINT LOUIS

Egypt or Syria, c. 1320–1340, brass, gold and silver inlay, diam.: max. 50.5 cm, height: 23.2 cm, former treasury in the Château de Vincennes chapel, entered the Louvre in 1832.

The wealth, diverse elements on the décor, and the brilliant craftsmanship of the master Ibn al-Zayn make this an indisputable masterpiece of Islamic art. Saint Louis, who died in 1270, did not bring this object back from the Middle East, but it was used as the baptismal font for the royal children of France, including Louis XIII.

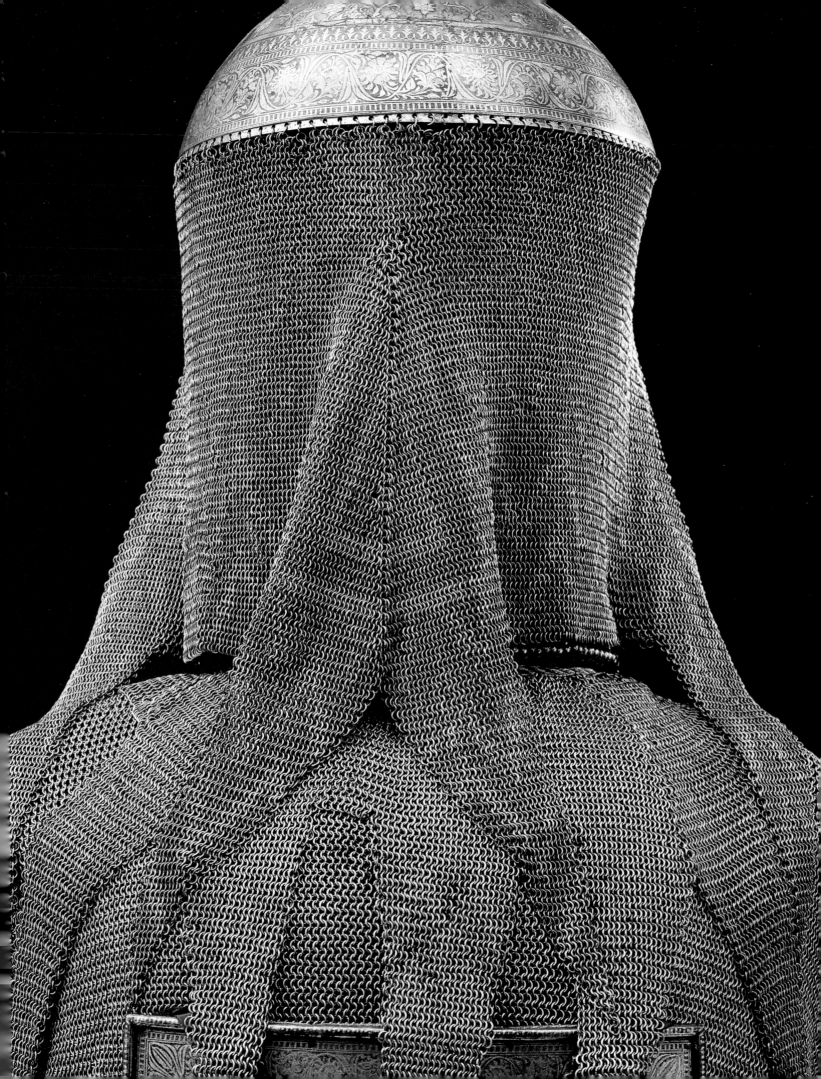

I. DAGGER FROM GEBEL EL-ARAK

Circa 3300–3200 BC. From Gebel el-Arak, south of Abydos, flint blade, ivory handle (hippopotamus tooth), length: 25.5 cm (handle: 9 cm).

This 25-cm-long dagger is a master-piece of Egyptian art from the pre-dynastic period. It consists of a carved flint blade and a delicately carved ivory handle. One side of the handle depicts a bearded figure standing between two lions. The other side carries a battle scene, deployed on two registers.

facing page

2. COLOSSUS OF KING AMENOPHIS IV

New Kingdom, 18th Dynasty, reign of Amenophis IV– Akhenaten (1353–1337 BC), Luxor, temple in eastern Karnak, painted sandstone, 137 x 88 x 60 cm. Gift from the Egyptian government for French assistance in saving the Nubian monuments, 1972.

This work illustrates the distinct and striking style of the early years of Amenophis IV's reign. As soon as he came to power, he constructed a temple in eastern Karnak dedicated to the cult of the solar god, Ra, whose visible manifestation was the disk Aten. This pillar comes from this temple.

Department of EGYPTIAN ANTIQUITIES

BY CHRISTIANE ZIEGLER
HONORARY CHIEF CURATOR

AND GENEVIÈVE PIERRAT-BONNEFOIS
SENIOR CURATOR, DEPARTMENT OF EGYPTIAN ANTIQUITIES

The Egyptian collection in the Louvre is located on the ground floor and upper floor of the Cour Carrée, where Jean-François Champollion, who brilliantly deciphered the hieroglyphs, set up the department and became its first curator in 1826. The layout designed by the architect Fontaine is still impressive, featuring splendid mahogany display cases with gilt bronze fittings, and sumptuous false marble and grisaille motifs inspired from the Egyptian civilization. The paintings on the ceilings were commissioned from well-known artists to glorify the land of the pharaohs. Still in place, they include François-Édouard Picot's *Study and Genius Showing Ancient Egypt to Greece* and Abel de Pujol's *Egypt Saved by Joseph*. The ground floor rooms are devoted to thematic displays of Egyptian civilization, while the art history rooms are on the upper floor. The Nile room introduces the Egyptian civilization, with images of the god of the Nile, boats, crocodiles and hippopotami, highlighting the importance of the river god in ancient Egypt. The delicate reliefs from the Akhethetep Chapel illustrate aspects of daily life and lead to rooms containing displays about agriculture, hunting, fishing, the home, leisure activities, hieroglyphic writing and intellectual life. A monumental granite sphinx in the center of this itinerary introduces religion, which starts with an Egyptian temple. Visitors discover sculptures re-creating multiple chapels, such as the Temple of Dendera, with the famous zodiac ceiling purchased for an astronomical sum by Louis XVIII. The monumental sarcophagi of Ramesses III, located in the Osiris crypt, introduces the world of the dead. The final section is devoted to the cult of sacred animals, with catacombs containing mummified crocodiles, cats and birds, as well as an evocation of the Serapeum of Memphis, where the sacred Apis bulls were worshiped. The North staircase leads to the upper floor and the start of the itinerary devoted to art history, presented in chronological order. More than four thousand years of history unfold throughout these rooms, from the famous *Seated Scribe* to the precious *King Osorkon II Pendant*, the brilliant blue faience hippopotamus, and *Sethos I's Encounter with the Goddess Hathor in the Valley of the Kings.*

Egyptian history continued uninterruptedly until the Romans conquered the Nile Valley in the first century AD. To discover this lesser-known period of Egyptian history, visitors must head for the Cour Visconti, with works illustrating the lavish history of the Roman Empire in the Near East and the Byzantine Empire. Egypt, which became a Roman province with the death of Cleopatra VII, nevertheless maintained a strong identity, as illustrated by the religious and funerary objects: sarcophagi and mummies; gilt funerary cartonnages; and large painted shrouds depicting the deceased under the benevolent protection of Osiris and Anubis. This encounter between two cultures is illustrated by the stucco masks featuring typically Roman headdresses and the spectacular series of "Faiyum portraits," rivaling the most beautiful paintings of Pompeii. Egypt was also one of the most brilliant and earliest centers of Christianity. The room devoted to the Bawit site is the only place in the world that presents such a representative display of the first Christian churches, as exemplified by the remarkable painting of *Christ and Abbot Mena*. Finally, tapestry art flourished during the Coptic civilization, as did sculpture, cabinetmaking and metalwork. An area devoted to antique Egyptian and Nubia in modern-day Sudan is currently under construction. The Louvre collection presents a vast overview of a multi-millennia civilization, whose masterpieces are an unceasing source of admiration.

LOWER GROUND FLOOR / DENON, SULLY

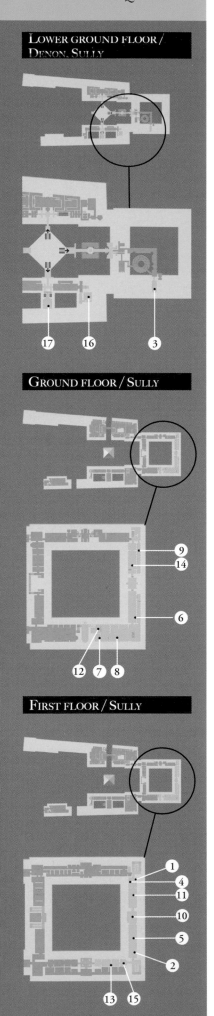

17   16   3

GROUND FLOOR / SULLY

9
14

6

12 7 8

FIRST FLOOR / SULLY

1
4
11
10
5
2

13 15

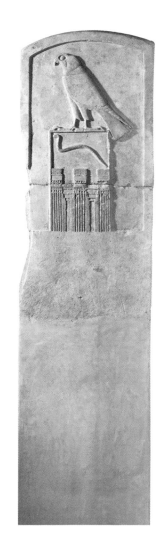

∧ 3. LARGE SPHINX OF TANIS

Old Kingdom, 2620–2500 BC, granite,
183 x 480 x 154 cm, 12 tons. Purchased as part
of the Salt Collection in 1826.

*The Egyptian sphinx, a monstrous being with
a lion's body and a royal head, is "the living image
of the king," who deploys his considerable strength
against the enemies of Egypt. This splendid
sculpture may date from the Old Kingdom
(c. 2600 BC), even though it bears the names
of several later kings.*

< 4. STELE OF THE SERPENT KING

1st Dynasty, c. 3000 BC, found in the king's tomb
in Abydos, limestone, remaining fragment:
143 x 65 x 25 cm, original height: 250 cm.

*The Thinite kings, who were buried at Abydos,
marked their tombs with these stone steles that
carried the first name of the deceased. The hieroglyphs on this monument read, from left to right:
"Horus, Serpent." The falcon is the god Horus, who
protects the royalty and its earthly representative,
the king. The serpent is a hieroglyph for one of the
king's names.*

< 5. SPOON WITH A YOUNG GIRL SWIMMING

New Kingdom, late 18th Dynasty, c. 1400–1300 BC, wood, sculpture in the round, 32 x 6 cm.

The beautiful, fragile work was probably designed as a work of art, rather than for everyday use. All the elements of this graceful sculpture—the highly erotic theme of the young nude woman, the pelvic area in the shape of a royal cartouche, and the Tilapia fish, a symbol of regeneration—must have given its owner great pleasure.

< 6. THE GODDESS SEKHMET

New Kingdom, 18th dynasty, reign of Amenophis III (1391–1353 BC), Karnak, Temple of Mut, diorite, 230 x 61 x 105 cm. Purchased from the Comte de Forbin, 1817.

King Amenophis III had several hundred sculptures of the goddess Sekhmet "the Powerful" carved for his temple located west of Thebes (modern-day Luxor). The engraved inscription mentions "Amenophis III, beloved of the goddess." These lines to the dangerous goddess were appeals invoking her protection for the country.

7. THE HARVEST AND TILLING THE SOIL

Painting from the tomb of Ounsou, 18th Dynasty, c. 1450 BC, left bank of Thebes, modern-day Luxor, paint on clay.

The paintings decorating the tomb of Ounsou, a scribe responsible for Amun's seeds, depict the agricultural tasks that Ounsou supervised in his lifetime. The composition, drawing, proportions, colors, and layout of the scenes, and the text itself comply with specific rules ensuring that the images would be as effective as possible in the afterlife.

< 8. CHAIR FROM THE FURNITURE DISPLAY CASE

New Kingdom, c. 1550–1069 BC, painted and inlaid wood, 91 x 47.5 x 59 cm. Former Salt Collection.

This chair, like the other objects in this display case, come from a cemetery near Deir el-Medina and date from the 18th Dynasty (c. 1450 BC), a period during which pieces of furniture that had been used in real life were placed in tombs. Egyptians stored their food in ceramic recipients and arranged their belonging in chests or baskets. They slept on low beds or mats on the floor. Chairs and stools, some of which could fold, were also common pieces of household furniture.

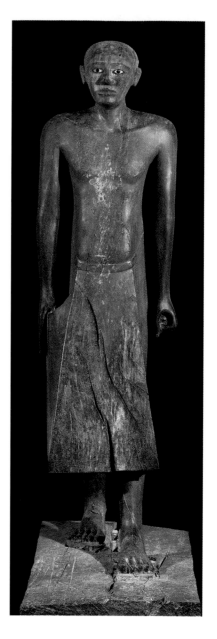

9. THE BOOK OF THE DEAD OF NEBQED

18th Dynasty (c. 1550–1295 BC), from Thebes, painted papyrus, 30 cm.

The "Book of the Dead" is a name created by Egyptologists to designate a collection of spells, placed with the deceased to help with the demands of the afterlife. The Egyptians called it the "Book of the Coming Forth by Day." It was written in the form of a papyrus scroll and varied greatly in size. The complete version included 165 chapters

10. STATUE OF THE CHANCELLOR NAKHTI >

Middle Kingdom, 12th Dynasty, reign of Sesostris I (1943–1898 BC), excavations at Assiut, acacia, 178 x 49 x 110 cm. Division of excavation finds.

Two alcoves were carved in Nakhti's tomb to house statues dedicated to his funerary cult, along with accessories to perpetuate the offerings. This work is exceptional, as it is life size and carved from fine acacia.

facing page

11. THE SEATED SCRIBE >

Old Kingdom, 4th Dynasty?, 2620–2500 BC, Saqqara, north of the avenue of sphinxes at the Serapeum, painted limestone, eyes inlaid with rock crystal and alabaster, set in bronze, 53.7 x 44 x 35 cm. Gift from the Egyptian government, division of excavation finds, 1854.

The "Seated Scribe" remains the most famous of unknown figures. We know nothing of the person it represents—not his name, titles or the sovereign he served. And yet his extraordinary face, with inlaid eyes, still astonishes visitors who discover it.

< 12. HIPPOPOTAMUS FIGURINE

Late Middle Kingdom, c. 1800–1700 BC,
silicious faience, 9.2 x 16.6 cm. Former Rousset
Bey Collection.

*The animal is covered with water lilies and aquatic
plants, as well as a bird in flight—a motif that for
Egyptians evoked the banks of the Nile, where the
animal still lived. To them, the hippopotamus
represented a refreshing image of nature, but it was
also a serious threat to the population and to crops.*

13. KING OSORKON II PENDANT: OSIRIS' FAMILY >

22nd Dynasty, c. 874–850 BC, gold, lapis lazuli and red glass,
height: 9 cm.

*This jewel is both a breastplate pendant and an amulet. It represents
the divine family, consisting of Osiris, his wife Isis and their son, the
falcon-headed Horus. Despite its small size, the object is one of the
best works of statuary from this period. It is one of many figurines
used throughout the first millennium BC, both in the world of the
living and in funerary practices.*

< 14. TAMUTNEFRET'S SARCOPHAGI

Third Intermediate Period, c. 1000 BC,
stuccoed, painted and gilded wood,
the largest sarcophagus: 192 cm.

*Tamutnefret, a singer of Amun, was a major figure
in the 21st Dynasty. She was protected for all
eternity against any hostile aggression, thanks
to the drawn and painted texts and images
covering the outer surface of her two coffins. She
rested within several coffins fitted one inside another, like nesting dolls.*

^ 15. RELIEF OF SETHOS I AND THE GODDESS HATHOR

New Kingdom, 19th Dynasty (1294–1179 BC), fragment of a wall from the tomb of Sethos I in the Valley of the Kings (Thebes, modern-day Luxor), 226.5 x 105 cm. Purchased by the Champollion mission, 1829.

The goddess Hathor greets the sovereign by taking his hand and presenting him with her emblematic collar, thereby placing him under her protection. In the necropolis of Thebes, the Egyptian capital during the New Kingdom, Hathor played the important role of greeting and accompanying the deceased into the afterlife.

< 16. CHRIST AND ABBOT MENA

Bawit Church, late 6th–early 7th century, paint on sycamore, 57 x 57 cm. Excavations, 1901–1902.

This small icon comes from the Bawit Monastery in Middle Egypt. It dates from the late 6th or early 7th century and represents Christ (easily identified by the cross within his halo) and Abbot Mena, the superior at the time. The abbot is holding a scroll in his left hand that may be the rules of his monastery.

^ 17. PORTRAIT OF A WOMAN

Egypt, Thebes, 2nd century AD, limewood painted with encaustic, 33 x 20 cm.

This type of portrait, painted on wood and known as a "Faiyum portrait," was placed over the face of the mummy. These painted portraits on wood did not exist in Egypt prior to the arrival of the Romans, who adopted the custom of mummification and introduced the use of the portrait. The woman's hairstyle, a soft braid wound around her head, was made fashionable by Sabine, Emperor Hadrian's wife.

Department of
GREEK, ETRUSCAN AND ROMAN ANTIQUITIES

BY ALAIN PASQUIER
HONORARY HEAD CURATOR

1. THE NIOBID CALYX KRATER

Attic, red-figure, attributed to the Niobid, c. 460 BC, terracotta, height: 54 cm, found near Orvieto in 1880. Acquired in 1883 (Tyszkiewicz collection).

This form of calyx krater was invented around the mid-6th century BC. This object illustrates the massacre of Niobe's children by Apollo and Artemis and was decorated using the so-called red-figure technique adopted by Athenian potters around 530 BC. The artist placed the figures in various registers in offset postures, a characteristic of the "severe style."

facing page

2. THE VICTORY OF SAMOTHRACE

Ex-voto from Rhodes commemorating a naval victory (perhaps at Side), early 2nd century BC, Paros marble (statue) and gray marble from Lartos (boat), height: 328 cm (statue with wings); 200 cm (boat); 36 cm (base). Found at Samothrace. Acquired in three different sections sent by Charles Champoiseau: 1864, 1879, 1891.

This composite monument of the goddess Victory on the prow of a ship stood in the sanctuary of the Great Gods overlooking the sea. Her large wings still seem to beat the sea air that blows her clothing against her powerful body. Her head and arms are missing, but her right hand, discovered in 1950, recreates the gesture of her raised arm commemorating the victory.

The Department of Greek, Etruscan and Roman Antiquities—along with the Department of Paintings—is the oldest in the Louvre. It is the direct descendant of the Musée des Antiques, which was included of the initial plan for the Muséum Central des Arts in 1793 and inaugurated in the Petite Galerie in 1800. It has always occupied the most historically important rooms in the Louvre. Initially, works were exhibited in the Salle des Cariatides, the original core of the Italianate palace conceived by François I. It also occupied the royal apartments on the ground and upper floors. Since 2004, the Louvre's former stables and the Salle du Manège have housed the antique sculptures from the collection amassed in Italy during the rediscovery of Antiquity. The destiny of this department took shape with the arrival of these latter works, acquired or seized by the armies of the Revolution and the Empire. They were added to the sculptures already acquired by the kings of France, Richelieu and Mazarin. The collection consisted initially of statues, relief sculptures and marble sarcophagi, vestiges of works by Greek and Roman sculptors. Other objects created from diverse materials—bronze, gold, silver, ivory, clay, mosaic and so on—then entered the collection. The galleries gradually acquired objects from the Mediterranean basin that spanned a timeframe of more than three millennia, through acquisitions initiated by government authorities and works sent to France from scientific missions and diplomatic initiatives, as well as through gifts and bequests. The department's collection therefore amassed a large number of objects, masterpieces and simple documents; the fine arts predominate, but archeology is also represented. The mission of the department is to illustrate the artistic creation and craftsmanship of the three so-called "classical" civilizations: Greek, Etruscan and Roman. Objects from ancient Greece are displayed in two different ways: rooms that place different techniques together (marble and bronze sculptures, painted vases, terracotta statuettes, etc), and others that present these same techniques separately. A mixture of techniques predominates in the gallery devoted to preclassical Greece—which presents the history of the Aegean world from the age of the Cycladic "idols" to the Archaic period—as well as in the ground-floor rooms.

The upper floor, on the other hand, traces the development of specific disciplines: the collection of painted Greek vases, for example, is one of the largest in the world. The rooms devoted to the Etruscan civilization present the art of this brilliant culture, including the *Sarcophagus of the Spouses* and the *Head of Fiesole*—from the period during which its art reinterpreted Greek forms until it blended into the crucible of Roman art. The distinct genres of portraiture, sarcophagi art, large mosaic paneling and metalworking are exhibited in the rooms devoted to Roman art. Three rooms on the upper floor house the Greek and Roman bronzes, precious objects with decorative bronze fittings, elements from the Boscoreale treasures, and finally, antique glass. The tall, powerful frame of the *Victory of Samothrace* stands atop the Daru Staircase, where she has been since 1883. Although the forms of classical Antiquity no longer exert the supreme authority they once did, this image of power and grace nevertheless continues to fascinate visitors from countries and civilizations around the world.

LOWER GROUND FLOOR /
SULLY

GROUND FLOOR / DENON

FIRST FLOOR / SULLY

< 3. HEAD OF A WOMAN

Fragment of a statue, Early Cycladic II,
c. 2700–2400 BC, marble, height: 27 cm, found
at Keros. Acquired in 1873, gift from Rayet.

*The Cycladic Islands were the center of
a brilliant civilization during the third
millennium BC. Marble female figures are
the period's most symbolic objects. The style of
this fragment, which comes from a life-size
statue, has been simplified, transforming the
figure into an abstract shape with a perfect
harmony between volume and line.*

4. SARCOPHAGAS: THE MYTH OF ACTAEON

Circa 125, marble, 99 x 235 cm,
found on the Via Labicana, near
Rome. Acquired in 1808 (Borghèse
collection).

*The number of marble sarcophagi
increased during the reign of
Trajan. The artist represented a
scene from the myth of Actaeon,
who stumbled on Artemis and her
followers as she was bathing. The
goddess transformed the young
hunter into a stag, and he was
then devoured by dogs. Shepherds
and women grieve for Actaeon on
the smaller panels of the coffin.*

5. FEMALE STATUE, KNOWN AS THE "LADY OF AUXERRE" >

Orientalizing style, c. 630 BC, limestone, height: 75 cm. Exchanged in
1909 with the Auxerre Museum.

*The influence of Near Eastern
arts on Greek art increased
during the 7th century BC. This
small statue, a goddess or orant,
was certainly made in Crete,
although it features an Egyp-
tian-style hairstyle. The accu-
rately proportioned figures and
volumes, as well as the colors
painted in the engraved decoration, bring this work to life.*

facing page

6. HEAD, KNOWN AS THE "RAMPIN HORSEMAN" >

Athens, c. 550 BC, marble with traces of paint,
height of the head: 27 cm (only the head,
which was discovered in 1877, is original).
Georges Rampin bequest, 1896.

*This smiling head is that of a horseman,
certainly a noble, wearing a wreath
commemorating his victory at the games.
The Louvre only has the head of this equestrian statue, one of the first of its kind in
Western art. The other fragments are in the
Acropolis Museum in Athens.*

∧ 7. HEAD OF FIESOLE

2nd century BC, bronze, height: 30 cm, found near Fiesole. Acquired in 1864. The head, cast using the lost wax technique, comes from a full-size standing statue.

It depicts a young man, with a rather heavy face and careworn features. His hair is extremely detailed, with full, precisely modeled strands. The artist paid particular attention to the individual features, prefiguring the work of Roman sculptors.

< 8. VENUS DE MILO

Circa 130 BC, Paros marble, height: 204 cm, found on Melos. Acquired in 1821, gift from King Louis XVIII, who received it from the Marquis de Rivière.

The goddess of Love, wearing a diadem and earrings, is half-nude with her weight resting on her right foot. The figure then defines several planes in space, a style common among sculptors since Lysippus. But the face harks back to features from the 5th and 4th centuries BC, identifying the work as neoclassical sculpture.

9. METOPE FROM THE TEMPLE OF ZEUS AT OLYMPUS >

Heracles and the Cretan Bull (detail), c. 460 BC, Paros marble, 114 x 152 cm. Gift from the Greek Senate in 1830.

This metope illustrates Heracles' exploit of capturing the Cretan bull. The overall work follows the labors of the hero, from the Nemean lion to the Augean stables, presenting a specific cycle for the first time. The sculpture is treated in high relief, according to a simple design: the two silhouettes intersect to form an "X" at the peak of their struggle.

10. SARCOPHAGUS OF THE SPOUSES

Late 6th century BC, terracotta, height: 114 cm, found at Cerveteri. Acquired in 1863 (Campana Collection).

This colorful sarcophagus, an illustration of an Etruscan funerary tradition, combines a coffin containing the remains of the deceased with a cover depicting life-size sculptures of the two spouses, united in death in a pose of banqueters. The woman, the equal of the man alongside her, offers her husband a bottle containing a fragrance.

< 11. GOLD PENDANT

First quarter of 4th century, gold, diam.: 9.2 cm.
Acquired in 1973.

This pendant was part of a larger necklace that included three other similar pieces. The coin in the center bears an image of Constantine, and was minted in 321; it commemorates the consulship of his two sons. It is set within a border of openwork gold leaf decoration that includes five busts (the sixth is missing).

12. RELIEF KNOWN AS DOMITIUS AHENOBARBUS

Circa 100 BC, marble, length: 205 cm. Acquired in 1824 (Fesch collection).

This bas-relief is the fourth panel of a group; the three others are in Munich. The Louvre panel illustrates an important act in Roman life: the census, which was necessary for recruiting soldiers. The event ended with a sacrifice of a bull, a ram and a pig to the god Mars.

13. PORTRAIT OF HADRIAN >

Second quarter of 2nd century, bronze, height: 43 cm. Acquired in 1984.

The exceptionally dynamic head of Hadrian depicts a severe face with a furrowed brow, softened by the curves framing his forehead and the short beard covering his chin and cheeks. This atypical portrait is one of the last images of the emperor.

< 14. SKELETON CUP

Boscoreale treasure, 1st century AD, gilder silver, height: 10.4 cm, found at Boscoreale. Acquired in 1895, Rothschild gift.

This cup was one of nearly 100 pieces of silver buried by its owners in Boscoreale, near Pompeii, during the eruption of Mount Vesuvius. The décor depicts skeletons named Sophocles, Zeno and Epicurus, performing a sort of macabre dance as they call on drinkers to seize the day.

^ 15. MOSAIC: THE JUDGMENT OF PARIS

After AD 115, mosaic, marble, limestone and glass, 186 x 186 cm. Acquired in 1932.

This mosaic pavement of an opulent home in Antioch. The central scene illustrates the myth of the judgment of Paris. In a mountainous landscape, Hermes asks the young Trojan prince, raised as a shepherd, to choose the most beautiful of the three goddesses: Hera, Athena or Aphrodite.

Department of
PAINTINGS

BY VINCENT POMARÈDE
HEAD CURATOR, IN CHARGE OF THE DEPARTMENT OF PAINTINGS

The Department of Paintings is in a class of its own, given its exemplary history, its constant commitment to exhibitions and publications around the world and, above all, the encyclopedia diversity of its collection. It aims to conserve and present technical and esthetic examples of pictorial art from the Middle Ages to the mid-nineteenth century, through nearly 7,000 paintings. It is a reference for the public at large, which visits the museum to admire the *Mona Lisa* and *Liberty Leading the People*, as well as for researchers, who can be assured of finding rare works and relevant comparisons—along with an exceptional documentation service. And it is, of course, a landmark for everyone seeking pure visual pleasure.

The Louvre's fame also resides in the coherent integration of government acquisitions and generous donations over the centuries. King François I started the Louvre's collection of paintings. The first masterpieces of Italian art, beginning with the world-famous Mona Lisa, became part of the French heritage through his well-chosen purchases.

The national painting collection was essentially formed by Louis XIV, who combined politics with a true personal interest in painting. By purchasing prestigious collections, including those of Cardinal Mazarin, Duc de Richelieu and especially the hundreds of paintings and drawings that belonged to the German collector Eberhardt Jabach, Louis XIV virtually single-handedly created the collection of French paintings: he was responsible for the purchase of thirty-one of the thirty-nine Poussin paintings currently in the Louvre. He also amassed the major works of the two other foremost schools in our museum: the Italian and the Flemish schools. At his death, the royal collection, which had only a few dozen paintings in 1650, numbered more than 2,500 works. The major initiative of the eighteenth century—particularly Louis XVI's reign—was the decision to allow the general public access to the paintings that had been dispersed throughout the royal residences. Furthermore, the museum acquired more than one hundred paintings from the Dutch school. With the creation of the Muséum Central des Arts in 1793, the conditions for expanding the national heritage changed, as acquisitions were financed by the government or received as donations from private collectors.

In the nineteenth century, Dr. La Caze bequeathed to the Louvre a number of seventeenth-century "painters of reality," along with eight works by Watteau, thirteen by Chardin, nine by Fragonard and a few Flemish and Dutch masterpieces. Paintings by Italian, Spanish and French Primitive artists were also acquired through judicious purchases. Similarly, works from less well-represented foreign schools were also purchased: the collection of works from the English school, for example, was formed almost entirely after 1900, while most of the works from the Scandinavian school were purchased after 1980. Visitors are still astonished by both the quality and diversity of the Louvre's three most important schools of paintings: the French school alone represents more than half of the collection (with approximately 4,000 works), followed by the Flemish and Dutch school (more than 1,400 works) and the Italian school (1,100 works).

The Spanish, English and German schools, which are represented with just over 200 paintings, as well as the Scandinavian, German, Austrian and Swiss schools, are still incomplete, which obviously points to one of the future aims of our acquisitions policy.

SECOND FLOOR /
RICHELIEU-SULLY

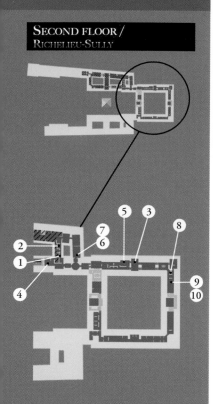

French paintings 16th-18th

1. JEAN CLOUET
(c. 1480/1540–1541)
FRANÇOIS I, KING OF FRANCE

Circa 1530, oil on wood, 96 x 74 cm.
Collection of François I, entered the
Louvre as part of the royal collection with
the creation of the Muséum Central
des Arts in 1793.

*King François I of French is represented
in a three-quarters pose, dressed in a
lavish Italian-style outfit. None of the
usual symbols of royalty—crown or scepter—was necessary, as the natural presence of the model fully expressed his rank.
This portrait is a perfect example of an
official royal portrait.*

2. JEAN COUSIN THE ELDER
(c. 1490–1560)
EVA PRIMA PANDORA

Circa 1550, oil on wood, 97 x 150 cm.

*By selecting a religious subject—to all appear-
ances Eve, the first woman—Jean Cousin
probably wanted to evoke the secular symbol of
the eternal woman and the universality of the
human conscience, over and above the eroticism
of the image.*

3. PHILIPPE DE CHAMPAIGNE
(1602-1672)

THE EX-VOTO OF 1662

Oil on canvas, 165 x 229 cm.

Champaigne painted this ex-voto in thanks for the miraculous healing of his daughter, Catherine, a nun in the Jansenist convent of Port-Royal in Paris. He portrayed the moment at which she was healed, with the mother superior, Agnès Arnauld, kneeling in prayer. The austerity of the scene underscores the profound spirituality of the painter and his models.

4. ENGUERRAND QUARTON
(active from 1444 to 1466)

THE VILLENEUVE-LÈS-AVIGNON PIETÀ

Circa 1455, oil on wood, 163 x 218 cm.

The action in this dramatic and expressive work is concentrated on the group of figures; it reflects the movement toward realism in France, as illustrated by the clear delineation and monumentality in the faces, draperies and figures.

THE CHEATER, Georges de la Tour *(c. 1635)*

5. GEORGES DE LA TOUR
(1593-1652)

THE CHEATER

Circa 1635, oil on canvas, 106 x 146 cm.
Acquired in 1972.

Born in Vic-sur-Seille in 1593, Georges de la Tour moved to Lunéville, in the Lorraine, in 1620. His themes included both humble people and religion, bathed in a sort of mystical darkness. During the Thirty Year's War, he speculated on grain and reproduced his works that were most in demand. His stylistic development demonstrates a strong influence from Caravaggio: the daytime paintings prefigure the pictorial vocabulary, limited palette and spare composition of his nocturnal scenes. La Tour died in 1652, but his son Étienne had already taken over his studio. Three accomplices are about to dupe an elegant young man, who is blinded by the dual temptation of gambling and erotic adventure.

Ⓐ THE PLAY OF HANDS

Card-players and gambling dens with their dangers and risky encounters were popular subjects, even though the church banned them. In this work, La Tour is certainly alluding to the biblical parable of the prodigal son, who squandered both his youth and his fortune. Three hands, those of the card shark and his accomplices, frame the glass of wine, a symbol of ill-fated intoxication. The index finger of the central woman is a sign of her impurity.

Ⓑ THE WOMAN'S EXPRESSION

The entire painting is organized around a surprising interplay of expressions, the language of the silent deception setting the stage to trap the victim. The woman in a red hat is wearing pearls, the symbol of venal love. She is not able to look the viewer in the face; the sideways direction of her almost black eyes reveals to us her duplicity. But unfortunately for her victim, he sees nothing.

Ⓒ THE ORANGE FEATHER

The colors—black, grays and bright reds—are also symbolic. The young man is dressed opulently; his eyes riveted on his cards (spades represent misfortune), he is unaware he is being cheated. This excessive sartorial display singles him out as the dupe. The naive-té of the deceived card player is evident right up to the bright orange feather on his hat.

6. CLAUDE GELLÉE known as CLAUDE LE LORRAIN
(1600–1682)
THE DISEMBARKATION OF CLEOPATRA AT TARSUS
1642, oil on canvas, 119 x 170 cm.

This work and its counterpart, "The Consecration of David by Samuel," also in the Louvre, were commissioned by Cardinal Angelo Giorio, one of Claude Le Lorrain's major patrons. The painter imbued this view with a mysterious poetry, applying all his knowledge of architectural composition and the depiction of reflected light.

7. NICOLAS POUSSIN
(1594-1665)
THE RAPE OF THE SABINES
Circa 1638, oil on canvas, 159 x 206 cm.

Romulus, standing on a platform, is overseeing the abduction of the Sabine women, who were to marry citizens of Rome. The painter wanted to create a realistic representation of the violence suffered by the women and the brutality of the soldiers; it is a powerful illustration of the classical ideal transposed to a painting.

8. JEAN-ANTOINE WATTEAU
(1684-1721)
THE PILGRIMAGE TO CYTHERA
1717, oil on canvas, 129 x 194 cm.

Watteau presented this painting, which ushered in the "fête galante" genre, as a reception piece to the Académie Royale de Peinture in 1717. It depicts lovers leaving for the pleasures of the Island of Cythera. This idealized landscape serves as a backdrop to the swirl of figures, underscoring the poetic world of this work.

9. JEAN-BAPTISTE SIMÉON CHARDIN
(1699-1779)
THE SKATE

1728, oil on canvas, 114 x 146 cm.

This was the painting that earned Chardin admission to the Académie Royale de Peinture. "The Skate" demonstrates his mastery in imitating textures and his skill in depicting inanimate objects. There is a mystery to this scene in the cat's expression and the gills of the fish, which look like eyes.

10. FRANÇOIS BOUCHER
(1703-1770)
DIANA RESTING AFTER HER BATH

1742, oil on canvas, 56 x 73 cm.

Rather than depict the image of a haughty goddess, Boucher chose to portray an accessible and graceful young woman, which heightens the sensuality of the scene. Boucher excelled in painting women's bodies; in this work he also proves himself as an animal and still-life painter, as well as a landscape artist.

6 4 2 1 3

5

French Paintings 19th century

11. JACQUES-LOUIS DAVID (1748-1825)
THE CONSECRATION OF NAPOLEON
1805–1807, oil on canvas, 621 x 979 cm.

Napoleon commissioned this immense composition, which includes 191 figures. A superb historical document, it is also David's crowning achievement in the art of portraiture, for the realistic depiction of the clothing and accessories and for the masterful spatial organization.

THE PROTAGONISTS OF THE SCENE

A – Napoléon I (1769–1821) is standing; he is the only actor on stage, among the passive spectators.

B – Joséphine de Beauharnais (1763–1814) is kneeling, in a submissive pose, as stipulated by the French Civil Code. She receives the crown from the hands of her husband, not the pope.

C – Maria Letizia Ramolino (1750–1836), Napoléon's mother, was placed by the painter in the gallery. In reality, she did not attend the ceremony.

D – Louis Bonaparte, (1778–1846): he was named Constable of France at the start of the Empire.

E - *Joseph Bonaparte (1768-1844): after the coronation, he received the title of Imperial Prince. He was named king of Naples in 1806 and of Spain in 1808.*

F - *Young Napoleon-Charles (1802-1807), son of Louis Bonaparte.*

G - *Napoléon's sisters*

H - *Charles-François Lebrun (1739-1824): Third Consul. During the First Empire, he was appointed arch-treasurer. He is holding the scepter.*

I - *Jean-Jacques-Régis de Cambacérès (1753-1824): Prince-Arch-Chancellor of France. He is holding the scepter of justice.*

J - *Louis-Alexandre Berthier (1753-1815): Minister of War, then Marshal of France; he is holding the globe topped with a cross.*

K - *Talleyrand (1754-1836): Named Grand Chamberlain on July 11, 1804.*

L - *Joachim Murat (1767-1815): Marshal of France, king of Naples after 1808, married to Caroline Bonaparte.*

M — *Pope Pius VII (1742-1823), merely gives his blessing to the coronation; seated behind Napoléon, but does not have either a miter or tiara.*

N — *Painter Jacques-Louis David is seated in the gallery.*

2. EUGÈNE DELACROIX
(1798-1863)
THE DEATH OF SARDANAPALUS
1828, oil on canvas, 392 x 496 cm.

This painting portrays the gruesome suicide of King Sardanapalus of *Nineveh, who decided to die rather than to surrender. This passionate, expressive, sensual and violent composition is considered to be one of Delacroix's masterpieces, a manifesto of Romantic art.*

3. JEAN-AUGUSTE DOMINIQUE INGRES
(1780-1867)
THE GRANDE ODALISQUE
1814, oil on canvas, 91 x 162 cm.

"The Grande Odalisque," the painter's masterpiece, was met with criticism at the 1819 Salon, before becoming one of the Louvre's most famous works, due to the delicate refined sensuality of the female nude and the realist rendering of the fabrics and accessories.

4. PAUL DELAROCHE
(1797–1856)
THE YOUNG MARTYR
1855, oil on canvas, 170 x 148 cm.

Paul Delaroche, a Romantic painter who was as famous as Delacroix in his time, chose to represent "the saddest and most sacred" composition in this lyrical scene. A young Christian girl is thrown into the Tiber River with her hands tied. It is an allegory of martyred innocence; the young girl brings to mind Ophelia, Hamlet's drowned fiancée. The tragedy affected viewers in the past, as it does to this day.

5. JEAN-BAPTISTE CAMILLE COROT
(1796–1875)
MEMORY OF MORTEFONTAINE
1864, oil on canvas, 65 x 89 cm.

This elegiac landscape is extraordinarily poetic and almost musical. Painted in a narrow palette of grays, greens and browns—Corot's famous "silvery light"—it presents a synthesis of his esthetic concepts and is one of the best examples of the "memory" genre as conceived by the painter.

6. THÉODORE GÉRICAULT
(1791-1824)
THE RAFT OF THE MEDUSA
1819, oil on canvas, 491 x 716 cm.

This painting was inspired by a tragic event: the 1816 shipwreck of the Medusa off the coast of Africa, and the endless ordeal of the 149 shipwrecked sailors on the raft—only 15 of whom survived. Géricault chose to depict a moment of hope, as a ship appears to save them.

FIRST FLOOR / DENON

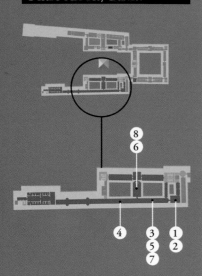

Italian Paintings

1. GIOTTO DI BONDONE
(c. 1267–1337)
SAINT FRANCIS ALTERPIECE

Circa 1295–1300, tempera on wood, 313 x 163 cm.

The altarpiece comes from the San Francesco Church in Pisa and represents four episodes from the life of Saint Francis. The largest depicts the saint receiving the stigmata, the marks of Christ's martyrdom, on his hands, feet and side. Giotto was one of the first artists to integrate realism, perspective, anatomical veracity and a sense of expression into his works.

2. GUIDO DI PIETRO, KNOWN AS FRA ANGELICO
(c. 1400–1455)
THE CORONATION OF THE VIRGIN

Circa 1430–1435, tempera on wood, 239 x 210 cm.

Fra Angelico painted this work for the altar of a church in the Dominican monastery of Fiesole. Six episodes from the saint's life are depicted around Christ arising from the tomb. This work, which radiates a deep and serene sense of piety, is one of the first masterpieces of the Italian Renaissance.

< 3. ANDREA MANTEGNA
(1431-1506)

SAINT SEBASTIAN

Circa 1480, oil on canvas, 255 x 140 cm.
Acquired in 1910.

Sebastian, a Christian soldier under the reign of Emperor Diocletian in the late third century, was sentenced to die. He was shot through by arrows, but was healed by Saint Irene. He would defy the emperor, who finally had him stoned to death. He was worshiped widely in the Middle Ages and the Renaissance; Mantegna, fascinated by Antiquity, paid particular attention to his depictions of sculptural fragments and architecture.

4. MICHELANGELO MERISI,
KNOWN AS CARAVAGGIO >
(1573–1610)

DEATH OF THE VIRGIN

1606, oil on canvas, 369 x 245 cm.

Painted for the Santa Maria della Scala del Trastevere Church in Rome, this work was refused by the clergy, who were shocked by the realistic depiction of the dead Virgin and considered it excessively realistic and theatrical. Caravaggio revealed his highly developed sense of drama and skill in expressing emotion in this painting.

< 5. RAFFAELLO SANZIO, KNOWN AS RAPHAËL
(1483–1520)
SAINT MICHAEL DEFEATING THE DEVIL
1518, oil on canvas, 29 x 25 cm.

Lorenzo dé Medici commissioned this famous work by Raphael in 1518 as a gift for King François I of France. It was probably executed by Raphael's workshop, perhaps by the most talented of his assistants, Giulio Romano. This masterpiece of balance, expression and movement had a profound influence on French painting.

facing page

6. LÉONARD DE VINCI >
(1452-1519)
THE MONA LISA, also known as LA GIACONDA
Circa 1503–1506, oil on wood, 77 x 53 cm.

The famous smile of Lisa Gherardini, the delicate position of her hands, the serene beauty of her face and the mystery of the imaginary landscape in the background all contribute to the fame of this universal icon—which has become the ultimate symbol of the Louvre. François I acquired the painting just after the death of the artist.

< 7. LÉONARD DE VINCI
(1452-1519)
THE VIRGIN AND CHILD WITH ST. ANNE
Circa 1508–1510, oil on wood, 168 x 130 cm.

The unusual theme of the Virgin sitting on the lap of her mother, Saint Anne, with the Christ Child, dates from the Middle Ages. Saint Anne embodies stability; her daughter, in a maternal gesture, is holding her Son. He has climbed astride a lamb, a symbol of his own sacrifice on the Cross. This painting is to religious painting what the Mona Lisa is to portraiture, through the purity of the landscape and the subtle rendering of the features.

following double page

8. PAOLO CALIARI,
known as VÉRONÈSE
(1528-1588)
THE WEDDING FEAST AT CANA
1562–1563, oil on canvas, 666 x 990 cm.

This painted was made for the refectory of the monastery designed by Palladio for the Benedictine Church on the Venetian island of San Giorgio Maggiore and is the largest work in the Louvre. It represents an episode from the New Testament: the moment when Christ transformed water into wine. The painter made full use of his exceptional knowledge of perspective and color in this composition.

SECOND FLOOR / SULLY

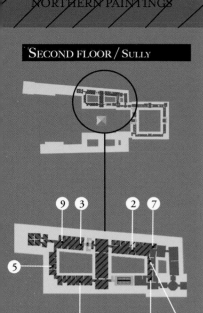

Northern Paintings
Flemish, Dutch and German schools

1. JAN VAN EYCK
(c. 1380–1441)
THE MADONNA OF CHANCELLOR ROLIN
Circa 1435, oil on wood, 66 x 62 cm.

The Chancellor of Burgundy, Nicolas Rolin, was an influential dignitary at the court of Philippe the Good. He is portrayed to the left of the composition, facing the Virgin who holds the Christ Child in her lap. Each detail is rendered with extreme refinement; this painting is also famous for the realism of the landscape in the background.

2. PIETER BRUEGHEL THE ELDER
(1525/1539–1569)

THE BEGGARS

1568, oil on wood, 18 x 21.5 cm.
Gift from Paul Mantz, 1892.

Five amputees seem to be preparing to go begging. An inscription on the back reads, "Courage, the maimed, salvation, may your lives improve." Is this a depiction of human suffering? An allusion to the festival of the beggars after Epiphany? The hats are carnival attributes, representing the various classes of society: the king (a cardboard crown), the soldier (a paper headdress), the bourgeois (a beret), the peasant (a bonnet) and the bishop (a miter).

3. PIERRE-PAUL RUBENS
(1577-1640)

THE VILLAGE FETE

Circa 1635, oil on canvas, 149 x 261 cm.

Several years before his death, Rubens returned to the theme of the village fete that developed with Brueghel. He added his own exuberance, lust for life and knowledge of composition, along with his famous vibrant colors. Louis XIV purchased this work for his collection.

4. QUENTIN METSYS
(1465–1530)

THE MONEYLENDER AND HIS WIFE

1514, oil on wood, 70.5 x 67 cm.

Quentin Metsys (ca 1465-1530) never abandoned van Eyck's legacy, but he introduced Leonardo da Vinci's style to painting in Antwerp in the early 16th century, which explains why his work features so many figures expressing—with strength or gentleness—a strong sense of sentimentality. The entire Flemish repertory—the *suffering of the Calvary, the unblemished kindness of the Virgin, the bluish landscapes with transparent hills—was influenced by Italian painting. Metsys' retables are powerful; his portraits, equally so. As a result, he was able to increase respect for the genre scene.*

This painting is a realistic portrayal of an everyday scene depicting a moneylender as well as a moral allegory: "May the scales be accurate, and the weights equal." This work speaks of avarice and condemns attachment to material goods.

THE MONEYLENDER AND HIS WIFE, Quentin Metsys *(1514)*

 A THE SCALES OF HONESTY

Each object in this interior scene, treated as a trompe-l'oeil, adds to the meaning of the scene. The apple placed on the highest shelf is the symbol of refused temptation, echoed by the more reassuring presence of the scale, the tool of the honest banker. The extreme care with which he tests the quality of good coins confirms his virtue, underscored by the gravity of his handsome face.

 B THE REFLECTION OF THE VIEWER

Like van Eyck and his portrait of the Arnolfini, Metsys placed a concentric mirror and his own reflection in this painting; its primary function is to double the space represented by adding that of the viewer. The volume is therefore complete, and the illusion contains the entire world. But this artificial eye, an element of the pictorial illusion, also suggests an external control on banking practices.

C MARIAN PURITY

The scene is made out like a double portrait or rather a diptych where the banker's wife replaces the traditional image of the Virgin. Even more than her white headdress, the book of Hours, from which she takes her eyes away for a moment, depicts her as a symbol of Marian purity. The painting wants to seduce the viewer while reminding the "good Christian" not to trade Heaven for the sole earthly goods.

5. REMBRANDT HARMENSZ VAN RIJN (1606-1669)

BATHSHEBA

1654, oil on canvas, 142 x 142 cm.

The painter chose to depict the precise moment at which Bathsheba, stepping out of her bath, receives a letter from King David asking her to be his mistress. This particularly moving and dramatic composition is an extraordinary example of pure painting, expressed through Rembrandt's thick, vivacious and sensual brushwork.

facing page

6. JOHANNES VERMEER (1632-1675) >

THE ASTRONOMER OR THE ASTROLOGER

1668, oil on canvas, 51 x 45 cm.

This famous work is the 32nd known Vermeer painting to enter a public collection. It may be a philosophical allegory or a specific portrait, but it is nonetheless a moving work in the precise rendering of the specific elements as well as the mysterious intellectual world it depicts.

< 7. ALBRECHT DÜRER
(1471-1528)
SELF-PORTRAIT
1493, oil on paper mounted to canvas,
56 x 44 cm.

The famous German artist made several self-portraits at different stages of his life. This is his first known self-portrait, probably painted around the age of 22. The symbol of the thistle in the painter's hand may be an allegory of conjugal fidelity or a symbol of Christ's Passion.

facing page

< 8. JOHANNES or JAN VERMEER
(1632-1675)
THE LACEMAKER
Ca 1665- 1670, oil on canvas, 24 x 21 cm

Vermeer painted interiors flooded with light, and limited the number of narrative elements, all of equal importance. The painter's brilliance derives from the extraordinary poetic qualities of his work, along with his meticulous technique and illusionism.

9. FRANS HALS >
(1580-1666)
THE GYPSY GIRL
Circa 1630, oil on wood, 58 x 52 cm.

The artist chose this "imaginary figure"—a prostitute, courtesan or Bohemian—as a pretext to demonstrate his technical brilliance. It belongs to a series of popular portraits created by Frans Hals in the middle years of the career and was inspired by the Bohemians or card-readers of the European "Caravaggist" style.

FIRST FLOOR / DENON

1
2

SECOND FLOOR / SULLY

3

Spanish Paintings

facing page

3. FRANCISCO DE GOYA Y LUCIENTES (1746-1828)
COUNTESS DEL CARPIO, MARQUISE OF SOLANA

Circa 1795, oil on canvas, 181 x 122 cm.

As a court painter, Goya was the favorite portraitist for Madrid's high society, a liberal milieu to which he belonged. Maria Rita Barrenechea (1757-1795), a playwright, had married Count del Carpio in 1775. The rigidity of the pose is tempered in this work by a profound psychological insight.

1. BARTOLOME ESTEBAN MURILLO (1617-1682)
THE YOUNG BEGGAR

Circa 1650, oil on canvas, 134 x 100 cm.

Rather than a mere moral or religious allegory, this realistic, moving and admirably composed genre painting belongs to a series by the painter depicting beggars or scenes of children.

2. DOMENIKOS THEOTOKOPOULOS, known as EL GRECO (1541-1614)
SAINT-LOUIS, KING OF FRANCE, AND A BOY

Circa 1585-1590, oil on canvas, 120 x 96 cm

This unusual style imbues form and feeling with the same passion: the extremely elongated hands and faces, chaotic perspective, flamboyant colors and strong brushwork. The retrospective image of Saint Louis, with the obligatory fleur de lys, has all the characteristics of a Mannerist portrait. The large patch of orange on the armor of God's soldier, matches the twisted body that occupies the space so powerfully.

Department of
SCULPTURES

BY GENEVIÈVE BRESC-BAUTIER

HEAD CURATOR, IN CHARGE OF THE DEPARTMENT OF SCULPTURES

1. DANIEL AMONG THE LIONS

Ile-de-France, early 12th century, capital, marble, 49 x 53 x 51 cm, from the Sainte-Geneviève Abbey in Paris.

The king of Babylon sentenced the prophet Daniel to be thrown in a pit along with starving lions, but he remained alive, fed by divine intervention. He is depicted in a seated, meditative pose, surrounded by two lions; placed in the corners, the lion's heads reinforce the structure of the capital, which is inspired from an ancient Corinthian capital.

facing page

2. DESCENT FROM THE CROSS

Burgundy, second quarter of 12th century, statue, wood with traces of polychrome and gilding,
height: 155 cm. Gift from Louis Courajod, 1895.

This Christ was certainly part of a "Descent from the Cross" consisting of several figures. The graphic folds in the clothing and the fine pleating falling in concentric semi-circles are characteristic of the stylization used by Romanesque sculptors. Painted wooden sculptures in France are extremely rare.

The sculpture collection originated with the upheavals of the French Revolution. There were so few sculptures when the museum was originally created (such as *Michelangelo's Slaves*) pieces confiscated from the royal collection, emigrants, churches and the Académie de Peinture et de Sculpture were sent to specialized institutions such as the Musée des Monuments Français (currently the École des Beaux-Arts) and the Musée Spécial de l'École Française at the Château de Versailles. The purchase of the Prince Borghèse collection in 1808 brought Italian Renaissance works to the Louvre.

Policy decisions, along with the closure of the Musée des Monuments Français in 1815, determined the location of a sculpture gallery on the ground floor of the western wing of the Cour Carrée, with works from the Renaissance to the present. Public commissions furnished neoclassical and romantic works; after the death of the artists, these sculptures could be taken from the Musée du Luxembourg, the antechamber of the Louvre devoted to living artists. It wasn't until 1850 that the first purchase, a medieval statue, entered the Louvre; and 1876 for the first expensive Italian work, the *Portal from the Stanga Palace*. Efforts by the Marquis de Laborde during the Second Republic and the early years of the Empire, followed by those of Louis Courajod in the last quarter of the nineteenth century, were decisive in establishing a coherent acquisitions policy. The aim was multiple: to form a lexicon of sculptors in the Louvre; to bring together disparate fragments from the Musée des Monuments Français; to create a collection that contained examples of all possible movements; and to exhibit the undisputed masterpieces of French sculpture. There were few major purchases in the nineteenth century, with the exception of the acquisition in 1863 of Marquis Campana's Italian collection. Instead, it was generosity of donors that brought additional works to the department, which was

separated from the Department of Antiquities during the Second Empire and the Department of Decorative Arts in 1871. In addition to generous donations (Davillier, Piot, Arconati-Visconti) and efforts by the Society of the Friends of the Louvre, sculptures were loaned from the collections of the Château de Versailles, the Monuments Historiques, the École des Beaux-Arts, the Observatoire and the Muséum d'Histoire Naturelle. In 1932, the department was transferred to the ground floor of the Pavillon des Sessions along the Seine, and expanded to include the Flore Wing, where it remained for nearly forty years. With the Grand Louvre project, outdoor French sculptures were moved to the Cour Marly and the Cour Puget (in 1993), and foreign sculpture to the Denon Wing (inaugurated in 1994). Medieval art is represented by fragments from the major centers of Romanesque and Gothic art purchased on the art market or transferred to the museum as religious buildings have been restored. Much of the funerary art, the art of the French Renaissance and seventeenth-century art came from the Musée des Monuments Français, which had, for example, acquired the best of Pilon and de Prieur's works. The Cour Marly essentially contains statues from the gardens of the Château de Marly-le-Roi that had been scattered among the various royal residences (primarily the Tuileries, along with Malmaison, Saint-Cloud and Versailles) before entering the Louvre collection. The eighteenth-century collection was formed chiefly by art collectors, but it also includes several series of commissioned works, with statues of public figures, for example. Large-format works and nineteenth-century sculptures, on the other hand, were transferred to the Musée du Luxembourg, while donations brought small bronzes to the museum. Finally, the collections of Italian and German sculptures were created primarily through costly acquisitions and the generosity of donors.

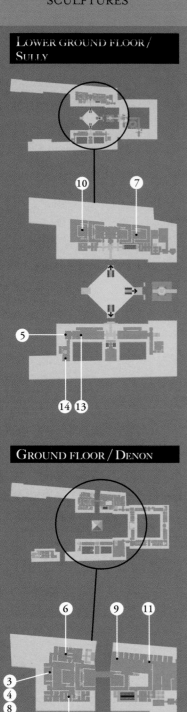

3. CHARLES V AND JEANNE DE BOURBON

Ile-de-France, last third of the 14th century, statue, stone,
height: 195 cm, from the former Salle des Antiques
in the Louvre.

*This image of King Charles V (1364–1380) and that of
his wife probably come from the façade of the Château du
Louvre, which the king remodeled. The smiling face of the
sovereign, known as Charles the Wise, illustrates the
development of portraiture art in the mid-fourteenth
century.*

4. TOMB OF PHILIPPE POT

Burgundy, last quarter of 15th century, group,
painted stone, height: 180 cm. Acquired in 1889.

*The funerary monument made for the Sene-
schal of Burgundy, lord of Roche-Pot, in the
abbey of Citeaux, is an extraordinary and
powerful monument. Philippe Pot lies atop a
slab borne by eight hooded mourners. Each one
carries an emblazoned shield, testifying to the
deceased's noble lineage.*

^ 5. BENVENUTO CELLINI
(1500–1571)
NYMPH OF FONTAINEBLEAU

1542–1543, high-relief, bronze, 205 x 409 cm. Confiscated during the Revolution.

The Florentine goldsmith was working at the court of François I when he designed this tympanum for the golden gate at the Château de Fontainebleau. It was ultimately placed at the entrance to the Château d'Anet, the residence of Henri II's favorite, Diane de Poitiers. In keeping with the Mannerist style, the nymph's body stands out against a background of animals drinking from her spring.

6. GERMAIN PILON
(known from 1535–1590)
DOMINIQUE FLORENTIN (died c. 1570–71)
MONUMENT FOR THE HEART OF HENRI II

Marble, height: 150 cm. Confiscated during the Revolution.

When her husband died, Catherine de Médicis commissioned this monument to hold the king's heart for the Celestine monastery in Paris. Germain Pilon sculpted the three Graces wearing rumpled draped robes, while Dominique Florentin created the base, inspired from antique altars.

facing page

< 7. PIERRE PUGET
(1620–1694)
MILON OF CROTON

1670–1683, group, marble, height: 270 cm. From the Gardens of Versailles.

Puget began this sculpture for the king in 1670. He was trying to express the cruel destiny of a hero vanquished by old age and torn apart by a lion, as his hand was trapped in the cleft of a tree. Puget achieved a technical tour de force by opening up large spaces in the block of marble, which add a dynamic energy to the composition's broad diagonal lines.

^ 8. MICHEL COLOMBE
(c. 1430–after 1511)
SAINT GEORGES SLAYING THE DRAGON

Circa 1509, bas-relief, marble, 128 x 182 x 17 cm. Confiscated during the Revolution.

The powerful minister Georges d'Amboise commissioned Michel Colombe to sculpt this altarpiece for the high chapel in the Château de Gaillon in the Eure department. The archbishop of Rouen wanted an image of his patron saint freeing the princess of Trebizond.

< 9. JEAN-BAPTISTE
PIGALLE (1714-1785)
MERCURY ATTACHING HIS WINGS

1744, marble, height: 59 cm.

From the Académie de peinture et de
sculpture.

*This is a "reception piece," a sculpture
required to enter the Académie de
peinture et de sculpture. In 1744,
Pigalle depicted the god of commerce
as he prepares to take flight. This work
demonstrates his artistic personality
through his understanding of Antiquity, as well as in the rendering of the
anatomy and movement.*

facing page

10. GUILLAUME COUSTOU
(1677-1746)
HORSE RESTRAINED BY A GROOM

Group, marble, height: 355 cm.

From the Place de la Concorde, 1984.

*Coustou sculpted two groups of wild
rearing horse, held by nude men, for the
horse-pond in the park of the royal
Château de Marly. In 1795, they were
placed at the entrance to the Avenue des
Champs-Élysées. Their fame is due to the
dynamic energy of the animals, modeled
after live horses.*

11. FRANÇOIS RUDE >
(1784-1855)
**YOUNG NEAPOLITAN FISHERMAN
PLAYING WITH A TORTOISE**

1833, marble, 82 x 88 x 48 cm. Royal
purchase.

*Rude, who created the famous
Marseillaise on the Arc de Triomphe
in Paris, made a preliminary study
of this figure—identifiable by his
hat, his net and his scapular—in
1829, and executed this work in
marble in 1833. He sought a natural
style, emphasizing movement and,
above all, a sense of joy.*

facing page

< 12 MICHELANGELO BUONARROTI,
known as MICHELANGELO (1475-1564)
SLAVES [DETAIL OF A GROUP OF TWO]

1513–1515, unfinished statue, marble, height: 209 cm.
Confiscated during the Revolution.

*Designed for the first funerary monument of
Julius II (1505) and executed for the second (1513),
the two slaves were never finished. Michelangelo
gave them to Roberto Strozzi, who in turn offered
them in homage to the king of France; they were
initially placed at château in Écouen, then the
Château Richelieu and finally Paris. We do not
know if they represent the arts reduced to slavery by
the death of the pope, or passions subdued.*

^ 13. DONATO DI NICOLÓ BARDI,
known as DONATELLO
(1386-1466)
VIRGIN AND CHILD

*1440, relief, polychrome and gilded terracotta,
height: 102 cm. Acquired in 1880. Donatello's
personality sums up the discoveries and inventive-
ness of the Italian Renaissance. The illusion of depth
is created by the seat in the foreground, and the
drapery background. Between them is the strong
image of a tragic Virgin, from whom the Child
turns away, as if with a premonition of the
Passion.*

14. GREGOR ERHART
(died 1540)
ST. MARY MAGDALENE

Early 16th century, polychrome limewood,
height: 325 cm. Acquired in 1902.

*Once known as "La Belle Allemande," Mary Magda-
lene is depicted nude, clad only in her hair. Erhart
depicted the Assumption of the saint into heaven,
drawing his inspiration from a Durer engraving.
Limewood was the favored material of Germanic
sculptors, who combined the influence of the Renaissance and Gothic traditions in their sensual modeling
of the body.*

Department of
DECORATIVE ARTS

BY MARC BASCOU

HEAD CURATOR, IN CHARGE OF THE DEPARTMENT OF DECORATIVE ARTS

This department presents a collection of extremely diverse shapes, materials and techniques covering a wide period from the Late Empire to the nineteenth century. Periods during which certain disciplines achieved particular renown are showcased. These include medieval enamels and ivories, majolicas, Renaissance tapestries and bronzes, and French furniture and precious objects from the eighteenth and nineteenth centuries. The inclusion of the decorative arts in the Louvre collection was planned from the inception of the Museum in 1793. Some one hundred objects from royal residences were transferred to the Louvre, along with vestiges from the treasury of the Sainte-Chapelle Church and the Saint-Denis Abbey. The small bronzes and precious stones from the former Garde-Meuble de la Couronne (Royal Furniture Repository) entered the museum somewhat later, in 1796. This first collection was expanded with the revolutionary and imperial conquests, as well as through a number of purchases. In 1802, when Dominique-Vivant Denon became director of the Muséum Central des Arts, the Department of Decorative Arts was not yet a distinct section, but was part of the Department of Antiquities. The acquisitions policy during the Restoration brought entire collections devoted to the Middles Ages and the Renaissance to the Louvre (Durand in 1825; Revoil in 1828). The treasury of the Order of the Holy Spirit was transferred to the Louvre after the order was abolished in 1830. The Decorative Arts collection expanded again during the Second Empire with the creation of the Musée des Souverains in February 1852, a project inaugurated by Napoleon III. It included historical works ranging from the reigns of Childeric to Louis-Philippe. Two large private collections entered the museum shortly after: the Sauvageot Collection (1856), consisting of medieval and Renaissance objects and the collection of majolica that belonged to the Marquis Campana (1861). After 1870 and the fall of the Second Empire, Émile Molinier opened a section devoted to seventeenth- and eighteenth century furniture, thanks to transfers from the Mobilier National, some of which had been confiscated from emigrants. When the Musée des Souverains was closed in 1872, the sculptures once again joined the Decorative Arts section. This situation prevailed until 1893, when the Department of Decorative Arts became autonomous. Gifts and bequests played a major role in the expansion of the collection in the late nineteenth century and first half of the twentieth century, both in terms of diversity within the entire collection and for the acquisition of individual objects. The first collections devoted to specific periods (Davillier, Arconati-Visconti, Rothschild) primarily concerned the Middle Ages and the Renaissance. But two bequests in the early twentieth century (Camondo, 1911; Schlichting, 1914) considerably increased the eighteenth-century furniture collection.

Other generous donors offered collections of faience, timepieces, snuffboxes and so on. After the Second World War, significant gifts made in lieu of inheritance taxes and several major donations (David-Weill in 1946, Niarchos in 1955, Grog-Carven in 1973) brought even more eighteenth-century works to the museum. Since 1966, the First Empire, the Restoration and the Louis-Philippe period have been increasingly well represented in the Department of Decorative Arts, forming a natural link to the Musée d'Orsay collection. The decision to move the Ministry of Finances in 1981 meant that the department could be completely rearranged to fully exhibit the magnificent collection. The new rooms devoted to the Middles Ages, the Renaissance and the seventeenth century, as well as the space set aside for the nineteenth century, including the lavish apartments created under Napoleon III, were opened to the public in 1993 and 1999.

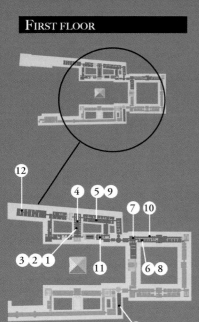

FIRST FLOOR

12
4 5 9
7 10
3 2 1
11
6 8
13

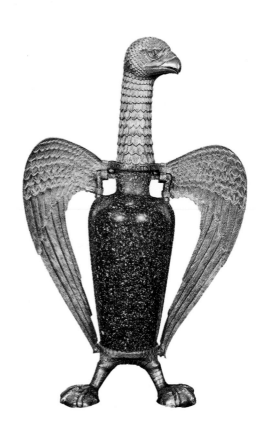

1. CHARLEMAGNE OR CHARLES THE BALD >

Equestrian statuette, bronze with traces of gilding. Late Empire (?) or 9th century, height: 25 cm. From the Metz Cathedral.

Inspired from antique equestrian statues, this statuette consists of three sections that were cast separately: the horse, the body of the horseman and his saddle, and the head of the horseman. The horse may date from the Late Empire, but the horseman—a portrait of Charlemagne or his grandson, Charles the Bald—is a rare example of Carolingian bronzework.

∧ 2. SUGER'S EAGLE

Vase: Egypt or Imperial Rome, mount: Saint-Denis before 1147, red porphyry, gilded silver, engraved, chiseled, and niello inlay, 43.1 x 27 cm. From the treasury of the Saint-Denis Abbey.

Abbot Suger (1122–1151), an advisor to King Louis VI and King Louis VII, undertook a series of renovation projects at the Saint-Denis Abbey. He had several magnificent liturgical vases made. Probably inspired by zoomorphic vases or Oriental fabrics, he commissioned this unusual eagle-shaped vermeil mount, placed on an antique porphyry vase. The strong naturalism of the bird's head and the extremely stylized plumage of this "eagle" prefigure Gothic art.

facing page

< 3. VIRGIN AND CHILD

Paris, c. 1260–1270, elephant ivory, traces of gilding and polychrome, height: 41 cm. From the Sainte-Chapelle treasury in Paris.

The growth of the cult of Mary in the 13th and 14th centuries led to the production of many figures of the Virgin and Child. This statuette is an unrivaled masterpiece of 13th-century ivory sculpture in the round. The slightly offset stance; the slender, supple figure; and the delicate triangular face, almond-shaped eyes, and smiling mouth are perfect expressions of the artistic canons of the time.

4. CHARLES V'S SCEPTER >

Paris, slightly before 1380, gold, gilded silver, rubies, colored glass, pearls, total height: 60.5 cm. From the treasury of Saint-Denis Abbey.

This scepter as part of the former regalia used during the coronation ceremonies of the French kings. The statuette representing Charlemagne atop a lily was clearly meant to link the power of the young Valois dynasty to the Carolingian history. The work is a magnificent example of the high-quality metalwork produced at the French court in the second half of the 14th century.

< 5. THE "MAXIMILIAN'S HUNTS" TAPESTRIES: THE MONTH OF JULY

Brussels workshops, c. 1530, after Bernard van Orley, wool, silk, gold and silver thread, 430 x 570 cm. Former royal collections.

The sumptuous Maximilian's Hunts tapestries were woven in the Brussels workshop of Guillaume and Jean Dermoyen from 1528 to 1533, from designs by the Habsburg painter Bernard van Orley. It is a masterful synthesis of Flemish narrative tradition and Humanist ideals from Italy. It represents scenes from hunts held throughout the twelve months of the year at the Brabant court. The month of July, illustrating the hunt of big game, depicts the moment at which hunters discover the animals' trail. The border combines garlands of foliage and small animals with allegorical trompe-l'œil friezes.

8. MARTIN CARLIN >

FALL-FRONT DESK

Paris, c. 1780, oak frame; veneer of ebony, rosewood, amaranth, fruit wood, aventurine, mosaic of marble and hard stone, gilt bronze, black enameled iron, Spanish brocatelle marble, 118 x 88 x 42 cm. Given in lieu of inheritance taxes, 1988.

This fall-front desk is the work of cabinet-maker Martin Carlin (c. 1730–1785). It was probably designed on order from a Parisian furniture dealer, perhaps Daguerre. The front, decorated with six mosaic scenes that seem to come from an older cabinet, reflects the revived popularity of colored stone in the late-18th century.

^ 6. ANDRÉ-CHARLES BOULLE

LARGE WARDROBE

Paris, c. 1700, oak frame; with ebony and amaranth veneer; marquetry of polychrome wood, brass and tin veneer, tortoiseshell, horn; gilt bronze, 255.5 x 157.7 x 58.8 cm. Former Baron Goguelat collection, given to the Mobilier National in 1870.

This wardrobe features a type of décor, known as Boulle marquetry, produced exclusively by luxury Parisian cabinetmakers in the latter years of Louis XIV's reign. This technique uses tortoiseshell and delicate metal inlays to form contrasting designs. Boulle, who by 1672 was working at the Louvre, created pieces of furniture that were renowned for their shapes as well as for the lavish decors of allegorical figures and ornaments.

facing page

7. GEORGES JACOB >

ARMCHAIR

Paris, c. 1777, carved and gilded walnut, 94 x 70 x 76 cm. Baroness Éva Gourgaud bequest, 1965.

This armchair was part of a set that was created in 1777 for the Comte d'Artois' Turkish Study in the Palais du Temple in Paris. The decorative motifs—cornucopias as arm supports, pearls and ropes on the armrests, doubles crescents on apron—were meant to reflect the exotic décor of the study.

11 >

9 >

< 10

< 12

9. ANGEL OF THE ANNUNCIATION

Deruta, 1st quarter of 16th century, faience with luster glaze, diam.: 42 cm. Former Campana Collection, acquired in 1863.

This large ceremonial plate is decorated with a scene of the Angel of the Annunciation in a landscape. The rim has a décor of flowers with an overlapping pattern. The piece has a beautiful metallic luster glaze, which is characteristic of luxury production in Deruta in the first half of the 16th century.

10. POT POURRI VASE

Sèvres, Royal Porcelain Factory, 1760, soft-paste porcelain, 37 x 35 cm. Acquired in 1984.

This pot pourri vase in the shape of a ship belonged to a set made in 1760 for Madame de Pompadour, King Louis XV's favorite, and delivered to her Paris mansion, the Hôtel d'Évreux, the current Élysée Palace. Charles-Nicolas Dodin painted the décor, which depicts an unusual chinoiserie scene against a pink ground, with blue and green highlights.

11. LÉONARD LIMOSIN
PORTRAIT OF THE CONNÉTABLE DE MONTMORENCY

Limoges, 1556, enamel on copper, giltwood frame, 72 x 56 cm. Confiscated during the Revolution (1794).

This painted enamel portrait of High Constable Anne de Montmorency (1493–1567), one of Henri II's friends and advisors, illustrates the skill of Léonard Limosin, an enameller who worked at the courts of François I and Henri II. He created the enamel-on-copper portrait that was so popular during the Renaissance.

12. FRANÇOIS-DÉSIRÉ FROMENT-MEURICE
HARVEST CUP

Paris, c. 1844, agate, argent partially gilded and enameled, pearls, 35 x 27 x 15 cm. Acquired in 1984.

This agate cup was inspired from Renaissance vases. Froment-Meurice, a famous silversmith and jeweler, created this piece for the fifth son of Louis-Philippe, the Duc de Montpensier. The mount consists of a vine stock made of vermeil that climbs up from a terrace and branches out to form a double handle.

13 a

13 b

13 c

13. CROWN JEWELS

The crown jewels are exhibited in the Apollo Gallery created by Louis XIV and decorated by Charles Le Brun, with additional work in the 18th and 19th centuries by such artists as Delacroix. They include the Regent [a], a 140-carat diamond purchased by Philippe d'Orléans; the Côte de Bretagne, a spinel cut in the shape of a dragon that once belonged to Anne de Bretagne; the coronation crown of Louis XV [b], now set with imitation stones; Queen Marie-Amélie's set of sapphire jewels; Empress Eugenie's pearl tiara [c]; and the most recent acquisition, in 2004, the jewels [d] given by Napoleon to Marie-Louise for their wedding.

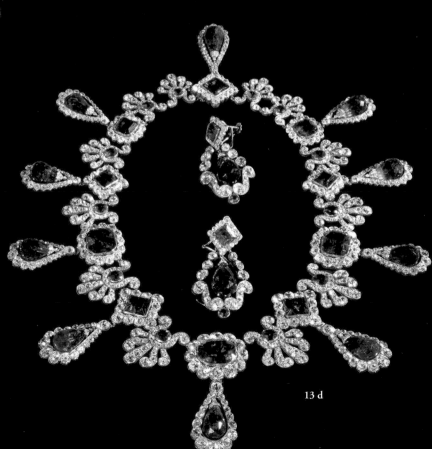

13 d

∧ 1. MICHELANGELO
BUONARROTI, known as
MICHEL-ANGE
(1475-1564)
CRUCIFIXION

1550–1557, black chalk, brown ink wash
with white highlights, 43.2 x 29 cm.
Acquired by the Cabinet du Roi in 1671.

*This drawing is part of a group of
studies, all the same size, on the theme
of the Crucifixion with the Virgin and
Saint John. The concise style and spiri-
tual intensity suggest they were made
late in the artist's career, between 1550
and 1557.*

facing page

< 2. MAURICE QUENTIN
DELATOUR, known as
QUENTIN DE LA TOUR
(1704-1788)
PORTRAIT OF THE MARQUISE DE
POMPADOUR

1755 Salon, pastel with gouache highlights
on blue-gray paper mounted on canvas,
177.5 x 130 cm. Acquired in 1838.

*This exceptionally large portrait is one
of the most spectacular pastels in the
Louvre's collection. The portraitist
satisfied his model's desire for an image
that corresponded to her role and her
ambitions. Jeanne-Antoinette Poisson
(1721–1764) married Charles-Guil-
laume Le Normant in 1741. Two years
later, she became the favorite of King
Louis XV.*

Department of
PRINTS AND DRAWINGS

BY CAREL VAN TUYLL
HEAD CURATOR, IN CHARGE OF THE DEPARTMENT OF PRINTS AND DRAWINGS

ARLETTE SÉRULLAZ
HONORARY CHIEF CURATOR

The Department of Prints and Drawings, which has been located in the Flore Wing since 1970, includes three different institutions. The first, the Cabinet des Dessins, was created from the former collection of the kings of France. It originated in 1671, with Louis XIV's purchase of 5,562 drawings that belonged to the most famous art collector of the time, the banker Eberhardt Jabach. By the late seventeenth century, the studio contents of the king's First Painters, Charles Le Brun and Nicolas Mignard, entered the Louvre. In addition to a few major acquisitions from the Mariette sale in 1775, the collection more than doubled with major revolutionary conquests and confiscated artwork—from the Comte d'Orsay, the Comte de Saint-Morys, and the Italian Dukes of Modena, among others. Frédéric Reiset was responsible for major acquisitions during the second half of the nineteenth century. In the twentieth century, the Cabinet des Dessins received monumental donations of works by nineteenth-century French artists. The department now has more than 140,000 works (if we include those with drawings on both sides), mostly covering the fifteenth to nineteenth-century French and Italian schools, with a significant number of works from the German, Flemish and Dutch schools. The second institution, the Chalcography, was created in 1797 to support the art of engraving by selling prints of the engraved plates collected during the Ancien Régime. Most of the copper plates came from the Cabinet des Planches Gravées du Roi, created by Colbert, and from the Académie Royale de Peinture et de Sculpture. The original collection grew throughout the nineteenth and twentieth centuries through these sales, as well as from gifts, purchases and commissions. Since 1990, the Chalcography has promoted contemporary creation by commissioning work from living artists. A third institution,

the Edmond de Rothschild Collection, created by James de Rothschild's son and bequeathed to the Louvre by his children, joined the Cabinet des Dessins and the Chalcography in 1935. In compliance with the terms of the donation, this collection has stayed together and remains a distinct entity. It consists of more than 40,000 engravings, approximately 3,000 drawings and nearly 500 illustrated books, including several incunabula. It provided the museum with an exceptional collection of Rembrandt etchings and eighteenth-century French engravings. The department's collection includes drawings, pastels, miniatures, prints, books, manuscripts and autographs—all fragile works that cannot be on permanent display and which require special conservation conditions. Works remain in the reserve collection and are brought out only for consultation purposes or for temporary exhibitions. These are limited to three months and are subject to stringent conditions: the lighting is limited to 50 lux on the surface of the object, the temperature-controlled environment is set to 20° C, and the relative humidity is 50 percent. The works are then returned to the reserve collection, where they remain untouched for three years. These exhibitions provide an opportunity to exhibit the collection from various perspectives; this diversity matches the historical, material and iconographic wealth of the collection. Since 1977, drawings from the second half of the nineteenth century have been part of the Musée d'Orsay's collection, yet the Louvre department continues to ensure the inventory and conservation of these works. The only works transferred to the Musée d'Orsay were the pastels, architectural drawings and decorative arts drawings, where they are exhibited on a revolving basis. The drawings can be consulted by requesting permission from the curator's office or at the main desk in the reading room of the Cabinet des Dessins.

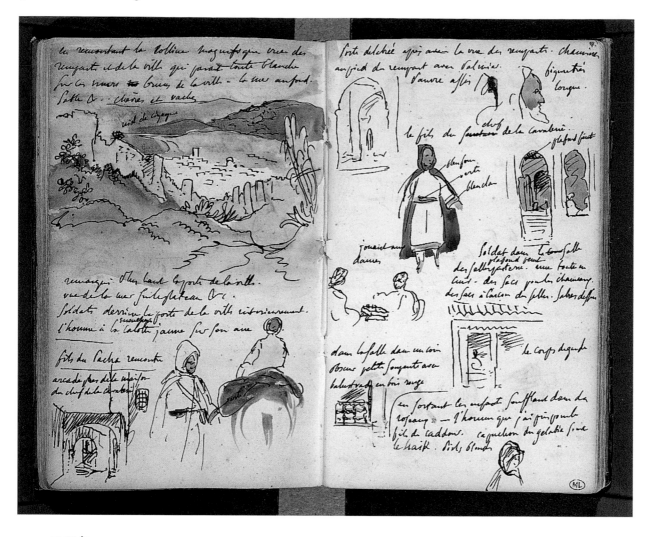

^ 3. EUGÈNE DELACROIX
(1798-1863)

VIEW OF THE BAY OF TANGIERS AND STREET SCENES

1832, folios 16 verso and 17 recto of a hardcover notebook covered
with green paper, consisting of 56 sheets drawn with graphite or
pen and brown ink, highlighted with watercolor and annotated with
handwritten notes, 16.5 x 9.8 cm. Acquired in 1983.

*After the occupation of Algiers in 1830, King Louis-Philippe
sent a diplomatic mission to the country led by the Comte de
Mornay, who asked Delacroix to accompany him. The artist
returned from his travels in North Africa with notebooks recording the intensity of his experiences.*

4. ANNIBALE CARRACCI >
(1560-1609)

WOMAN CARRYING A BASKET ON HER HEAD

Circa 1597, black chalk and white highlights on
gray-white paper, 42.6 x 28.8 cm. A.-Ch. His de
la Salle bequest in 1878.

*This is a study for the woman who appears to
the right in the fresco in the center of the vault
of the Farnese Gallery in Rome: "The Triumph
of Bacchus and Ariadne," Annibale Carracci's
masterpiece. He began working on the ceiling
in 1597.*

5. LEONARDO DA VINCI
(1452-1519)
PORTRAIT OF ISABELLA D'ESTE

Circa 1499–1500, black and red chalk with golden yellow
pastel highlights on cardboard, 36 x 46 cm, pricked for transfer.
Acquired in 1860.

*Leonardo made this cartoon during a trip to Mantua in
December of 1499, in preparation for a portrait commissioned
by Isabella d'Este (1474–1539). Despite repeated requests,
the painting was never executed. The placement of the hands
foreshadows that of the "Mona Lisa."*

6. REMBRANDT HARMENSZ VAN RIJN
(1606-1669)
**CHRIST HEALING THE SICK, ALSO KNOWN AS THE HUN-
DRED GUILDER PRINT**

Circa 1642–1649, etching, drypoint and burin, proof from the
first state, 27.8 x 38.8 cm. Edmond de Rothschild Collection,
bequeathed in 1935.

*Drypoint creates a light line, while the burin added velvety
black tones. The name "Hundred Guilder Print" commonly
used for this famous and unusually large etching, comes from
the high price it commanded as early as the 17th century.*

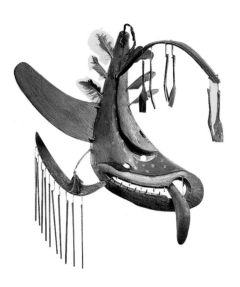

The Pavillon des Sessions

SCULPTURES FROM AFRICA, ASIA, OCEANIA AND THE AMERICAS

BY GERMAIN VIATTE
HONORARY CHIEF CURATOR

above

1. YUP'IK (INUIT) SCULPTURE

White whale and swan mask, Napaskiak village, region of the Kuskokwim River, Alaska, early 20th century, polychrome wood, feathers, height: 72 cm. Work collected by Adams Hollis Twitchell, 1908. The Museum of the American Indian, Heye Foundation, New York. Former André Breton Collection. Musée du quai Branly.

Collected in 1908, this mask was exhibited at the Museum of the American Indian in New York. The Surrealists loved the poetry of this work. It was used in ceremonies to assist with the hunt for the white whale, one of the primary resources of the Inuit. The swan was an intermediary between man and the animal.

Since the spring of 2000, the Musée du Louvre has exhibited 120 masterpieces from the continents of Africa, Asia, Oceania and the Americas. This fresh look at other art forms and other traditions is intended to help form "new relationships based on comprehension, mutual respect, dialogue and exchange," in the words of the French president of the Republic, Jacques Chirac, and goes beyond the goals outlined for the creation of the Grand Louvre. This exhibition affirms the "equality of cultures" within this great museum, by showcasing the longstanding history of these civilizations, as well as the fascination and influence they exert on our own.

This selection of works is an extension to the Musée du quai Branly, which has opened in June 2006. This new building houses the national collections of art and ethnology that had previously been in the Musée de l'Homme and the Musée National des Arts d'Afrique et d'Océanie. This anthology of exceptional works was curated by Jacques Kerchache. It is devoted exclusively to the art of sculpture and stresses the formal invention of the artists. The exhibition includes loans of works from several countries of origin and well as from French museums. It underscores the professional and cultural links that will be established in the future between these different participants.

< 1. SCULPTURE FROM EASTER ISLAND

MOAI HEAD

Anakena Bay, Easter Island, 11th-15th century, volcanic tuff, height: 170 cm. Gift from the Chilean government, 1935. Musée du Quai Branly.

The "Moai" were carved from the soft rock of the Rano Raraku volcano. The head represents nearly two-fifths the size of the sculpture, which was about five meters high. It probably depicts a god or the ancestor of a family group, raised to the status of a deity. It was placed on a ceremonial platform called an "Ahu"—a sanctuary and ossuary for the clan.

2. TAINO SCULPTURE CEREMONIAL THRONE (DUHO) >

IIsland of Hispaniola (Haiti and Dominican Republic), Greater Antilles, 14th century, guayac wood, 42 x 30.3 cm. Gift from David Weill to the Musée de l'Homme, 1950. Musée du quai Branly.

The Taino were the first American Indians encountered by the Spanish conquistadores, but they disappeared within just a few decades. During the many rituals that accompanied their lives, the ceremonial wooden seat, emblematic of power, was reserved to the chief. It represented a zemi, a deity linked to the world of the spirits.

GROUND FLOOR / DENON

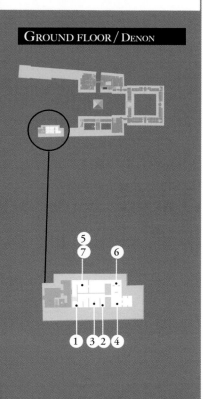

4. KORWAR SCULPTURE

Reliquary, Geelvink Bay, Irian Jaya (Western New Guinea), late 18th century, wood, skull, glass beads, height: 55 cm. Work collected during the Duperrey expedition in 1824. Former Lesson and Garnot Collection, Musée d'Ethnographie du Trocadéro since 1885. Musée du Quai Branly.

This sculpture, certainly created by a shaman, was discovered in 1824 in the northwest area of New Guinea. Very few European collections have a "korwar" sculpture with a skull. Most of these reliquaries, which are receptacles for the spirit of the deceased, were made entirely of wood. They offered protection and were also used as oracles.

5. SCULPTURE DEDICATED TO GOU, GOD OF WROUGHT IRON AND WARFARE

Work created before 1858 by Akati Ekplékendo, a Fen artist from Doumé, Republic of Benin, iron, wood, height: 165 cm. Gift from Captain Eugène Fonssagrives to the Musée d'Ethnographie du Trocadéro, 1894. Musée du Quai Branly.

The large figure of the god Gou was brought to France in the late 19th century after the conquest of Dahomey. It is astonishingly modern and is unique in the history of African sculpture. The figure carries a ceremonial saber and an iron altarpiece on its head, with attributes representing its status as a god of wrought iron and warfare.

6. SCULPTURE FROM THE NORTH OF NIAS ISLAND

Ancestral statue (adu zatua), Indonesia, 19th century, wood, crusty red patina, height: 55,7 cm. Former collections of André Breton, Helena Rubinstein and Alain Schoffel. Gift from Alain Schoffel, 1999. Musée du Quai Branly.

André Breton had just acquired this work when it was shown in Paris, in 1925, as part of the "Man Ray et objets des îles" exhibition. Called "adu zatua," the ancestral statuettes of Nias were made by master sculptors. The tall headdresses decorated with ferns and the decoration indicated their social rank.

7. SAPI SCULPTURE >

Tusk, Sierra Leone, 15th–16th century, ivory, length: 79 cm. Former Bibliothèque nationale de France Collection, Cabinet des Médailles, Paris. Musée du Quai Branly.

This finely carved horn is emblematic of the so-called "Sapi-Portuguese ivories" made for export. They combine African symbolism with European designs. Viewed as both an art object and "exotic curiosity," it belonged to the royal collection prior to the French Revolution.

Museum
EUGÈNE DELACROIX

BY ARLETTE SÉRULLAZ
HONORARY CHIEF CURATOR

The Eugène Delacroix Museum has been affiliated with the Musée du Louvre since January 2004 and is housed in the artist's Paris apartment at 6 Rue de Furstenberg, where he lived from 1858 to his death in 1863. The visit begins with the three rooms of the apartment open to the public: the bedroom, the sitting room and the library. The dining room is currently being used as the museum's documentation center. Delacroix had been living on Rue Notre-Dame-de-Lorette since 1844. Étienne Haro, who sold materials to the artist, found an apartment closer to the Saint-Sulpice Church, where Delacroix had been working on a commission for one of the chapels. The many advantages of this new apartment—including the possibility of constructing a studio in the garden and the charm of the countryside in the heart of Paris—were greater than the inconveniences caused by yet another move.

After Delacroix died, the Saint-Vincent-de-Paul company rented the apartment and studio. In 1928, the building's owner, Charles Panckoucke, gave notice that he was terminating the lease. Two painters, Maurice Denis and Paul Signac, were worried about the future of the studio and formed a Society of the Friends of Delacroix. They were supported by the City of Paris and managed to collect enough money to rent the studio and the apartment. Until 1952, this society organized exhibitions, conferences and concerts. Panckoucke died and the building was put up for sale. The Society of the Friends of Delacroix was unable to intervene and turned for help to the government in exchange for a selection of works by Delacroix. Thanks to the considerable generosity of M. David David-Weill, it was able to purchase the apartment and studio, which were then donated in 1956 to the government, to be transformed into a public museum. In 1971, the Eugène Delacroix Museum became a national museum. The Society of the Friends of Delacroix was dissolved in 2000 and was replaced by a Society of the Friends of the Museum. One of their first acts was to give the entire collection of works inherited from the former Society to the French government. In the last twenty years, the museum has pursued an active acquisitions policy. Major works have entered the collection, which consists of paintings, drawings, engravings, letters and memorabilia that belonged to the painter, his family, his friends and his fellow artists—as well as all the objects Eugène Delacroix brought back from his trip to North Africa.

EUGÈNE DELACROIX
(1798-1863)
PORTRAIT OF THE ARTIST
Oil on canvas, 65 x 54 cm.
Musée du Louvre.

Born in 1798 to a cultivated bourgeoise family, Delacroix was the leading figure of the Romantic movement. He was considered one of the greatest artists of his century and published his theories on color. The Louvre has 67 of his canvases, including his major works: "Dante's Boat," "The Death of Sardanapalus," "Liberty Leading the People" and "The Massacre at Chios."

PRACTICAL INFORMATIONS

ADMISSION

Entrance to the permanent and temporary exhibitions at the Louvre Museum (including entrance to the Eugène Delacroix Museum).

Tickets

Permanent collection: 9 € full price; 6 € reduced rate, Wednesday and Friday after 6 pm.

Specific tickets

Exhibitions in the Napoleon Hall: 8.50 €.

Combined tickets

Permanent collection and exhibitions in the Napoleon Hall: 13 € full price. 11 € reduced rate, Wednesday and Friday after 6 pm.

Free admission

Admission to the Louvre Museum and to the Eugène Delacroix Museum is free, on presentation of a valid proof of identity, for:
- visitors under 18 years old
- visitors under 26 years old every Friday evening after 6 pm (excluding exhibitions in the Napoleon Hall)
- unemployed and recipients of minimum social benefits
- disabled visitors and the accompanying person
- art history instructors (on presentation of a card indicating the subject taught) and applied arts instructors
- all visitors, all day, the first Sunday of every month

Admission is free for Louvre Jeune, Louvre Professionnels, Louvre enseignants, Friends of the Louvre cardholders, as well as art students and students from participating institutions with passes.

USEFUL INFORMATION

Access: métro Palais Royal/Musée du Louvre (line 1 or 7).

Tel: 01 40 20 50 50.

Information desk: 01 40 20 53 17.

Website: www.louvre.fr

Opening hours

The museum is open 9 am to 6 pm; closed Tuesday and holidays. Ticket windows close at 5:15 pm. The museum rooms close starting at 5:30 pm.

Late-night opening hours

Three wings of the museum (Denon, Sully et Richelieu) are open Wednesday and Friday night until 9:45 pm. The ticket windows close at 9:15 pm. The rooms start closing at 9:30 pm. The Louvre's historical rooms are open Monday 9 am to 6 pm.

Free facilities

Cloakroom for coats and small bags, loan of strollers and wheelchairs, first aid, lost and found.

Headphones

available in six languages. Rentals at the Denon, Sully and Richelieu entrances (on the mezzanine under the pyramid). Price: 5 €.

reservations: 01 47 51 60 06.

To avoid lines, buy your ticket in advance

> Individual tickets (less than 20)

Tickets valid for the permanent collection and/or temporary exhibitions, with direct access via the Passage Richelieu or the Galerie du Carrousel.
- in these stores: Fnac, Carrefour, Continent, Auchan, Extrapole, Le Bon Marché, Le Printemps, Galeries Lafayette, BHV, Virgin Megastore, Leclerc
- by telephone:
Fnac: 0 892 684 694 or
Ticket Net: 0 892 697 073
- on the web: www.louvre.fr
- in regional train stations, zones 1 to 6, SNCF Ile-de-France (transportation + admission)
- at the Paris tourist office (billet Louvre-RATP) 0 892 683 000, www.paris-touristoffice.com

> To purchase 20 or more tickets

Boutiques Musée & Compagnie, 49, rue Étienne-Marcel, 75001 Paris
Tel: 01 40 13 49 13.
Advance-purchase tickets are valid for an unlimited period.

To purchase tickets to the Louvre Auditorium

> Information

01 40 20 55 55 (Monday to Friday, 9 am to 7 pm).
www.louvre.fr

> Reservations

By telephone: 01 40 20 55 00 (payment by credit card).

At the auditorium ticket window Monday, Wednesday, Thursday, Friday: 9 am to 7:30 pm; Saturday: 9 am to 5:30 pm.

Workshops and tours

Various options are available for museum visitors: lecture/tours, architectural itineraries, workshops for children and adults.
Information: 01 40 20 52 63.

Group tours

Reservations required.
Reservation with a museum lecturer: tel: 01 40 20 51 77; fax: 01 40 20 84 58.
Reservation with a non-Louvre guide or lecturer: tel: 01 40 20 57 60; fax: 01 40 20 58 24.

Disabled visitors

Information: 01 40 20 59 90.
handicap@louvre.fr
Information and maps in French and English are available for disabled visitors at the information desk (under the pyramid). Wheelchairs are available free of charge. To visit the Eugène Delacroix Museum, tel: 01 44 41 86 50.

CyberLouvre

The CyberLouvre, located in the avenue of the Grand-Louvre, presents the Louvre's multimedia resources, CD-ROMs, database and the cultural Internet. There are people on hand to assist visitors. This area is located in the passage linking the Hall Napoleon to the Galerie du Carrousel; entrance is free. Open daily, except Tuesday and certain public holidays, 9 am to 5:45 pm.
Tel: 01 40 20 67 30.
The CyberLouvre is sponsored by Daï Nippon Printing.

BECOME A MEMBER

Join the Friends of the Louvre Association

The Friends of the Louvre Association is independent from the Louvre Museum. Benefits include free admissions to the museum and to temporary exhibitions.

Individual membership: 01 40 20 53 34 / 53 74.

Group membership: 01 40 20 84 94.

Friends of the Louvre information:

01 40 20 53 34 or 01 40 20 53 74

www.amis-du-louvre.org

The Friends of the Louvre desk is located in the Galerie du Carrousel (Avenue du Grand-Louvre); open daily except Tuesday and Sunday, 10 am to 5:30 pm.

Louvre passes

The Louvre proposes various passes, available in the new "membership area." Daily, except Tuesday, 9 am to 5:15 pm; to 9:15 when the museum is open late.
Tel: 01 40 20 51 04.

To download application forms: www.louvre.fr

Carte Louvre jeunes

For under 26-year-olds.
adhesion.louvrejeunes@louvre.fr

Carte Louvre enseignants (for teachers)

louvreenseignants@louvre.fr

Carte Louvre professionnels (for professionals)

louvreprofessionnels@louvre.fr

MUSÉE DU LOUVRE

President and Director of the Louvre Museum
Henri Loyrette

General Manager of the Louvre Museum
Didier Selles

Assistant General Manager
Catherine Sueur

Publications
Violaine Bouvet-Lanselle, head of the publications department, coordinated this project, including supervision of the texts and illustrations.

The introductory text and commentaries for the Department of Islamic Art were written in conjunction with Cécile Jail, responsible for documentary research in the Department of Islamic Art; those for the Egyptian Antiquities were written, in part, by Geneviève Pierrat-Bonnefois, head curator of the Department of Egyptian Antiquities.

The documentation for the commentaries for the Pavillon des Session artwork (African and Oceanic arts) was provided by Marine Degli, curator and exhibition assistant at the Musée du quai Branly.

Thanks to

Muriel Rausch, Roberta Cortopassi, Carole Nicolas, Catherine Dupont, Marie-Claire Guillard Le Bourdellès, Cédric Beal, Erich Lessing, Alice Ertaud.

© Musée du Louvre, 2005

ISBN MUSÉE DU LOUVRE : 978-2-35031-160-9

EDITIONS BEAUX ARTS

This guide is published by Beaux Arts / TTM Éditions.

This special issue was co-published with the Louvre Museum.

Beaux Arts éditions
86, rue Thiers
92100 Boulogne-Billancourt
Tél. +33 (1) 41 41 55 60
Fax: +33 (1) 41 41 98 35
RCS Paris B 435 355 869

Dépôt légal: October 2007

Photoengraving: Lithoart, Turin
Printer: Clerc, Saint-Amand-Montrond
Printed in France

Publisher Thierry Taittinger

Editor Claude Pommereau

Financial and administrative director
Thierry Lalande

Publication director and editor-in-chief
Fabrice Bousteau

Editorial assistant Catherine Joyeux

Partnerships and Senior editor
Jean-Christophe Claude

Editor Séverine Cuzin

Product manager Laure Boutouyrie

Design Stéphane Argillet

Picture editors: Alexandra Buffet, Julie Le Borgne

Copy editors Malika Bauwens, Sabine Moinet

Translator Lisa Davidson

Distribution Florence Hanappe, tél. +33 (1) 41 41 55 77

Accounts
Cabinet Lourdeau, 55 rue de l'Université, 75007 Paris tél. 01 53 63 04 88

© Beaux Arts/TTM Éditions, 2007

ISBN BEAUX ARTS : 978-2-84278-595-6

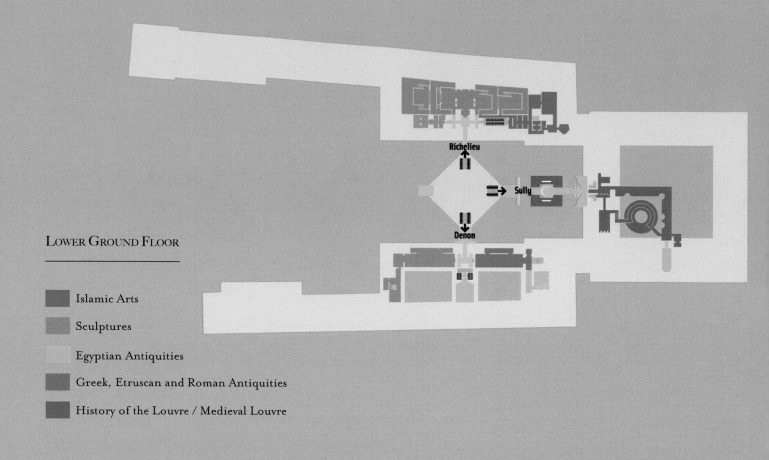

Lower Ground Floor

- Islamic Arts
- Sculptures
- Egyptian Antiquities
- Greek, Etruscan and Roman Antiquities
- History of the Louvre / Medieval Louvre

Richelieu

Sully

Denon

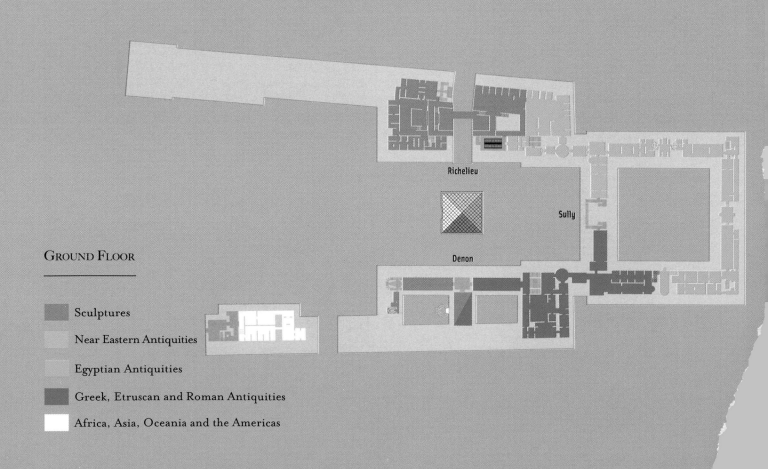

Richelieu

Sully

Denon

Ground Floor

- Sculptures
- Near Eastern Antiquities
- Egyptian Antiquities
- Greek, Etruscan and Roman Antiquities
- Africa, Asia, Oceania and the Americas